D1356709

Faith and Spirituality
Loughborough University

Soups *from a* Monastery Kitchen

Soups *from a* Monastery Kitchen

Twelve Months of International Favourites

Brother
Victor-Antoine

Arcadia

Copyright © 1996 by Brother Victor-Antoine d'Avila Latourette. First published under the title Twelve Months of Monastery Soups by Liguori/Triumph, an imprint of Liguori Publications, Liguori, Missouri, USA.

This edition published by Arcadia Publishing Services Ltd, 2A Endeavour House, 2 Cambridge Road, Kingston-upon-Thames, Surrey KT1 3JU.

British Library Cataloguing in Publication Data. A catalogue record for this book is available from the British Library.

All rights reserved. No part of this publication may be reproduced or transmitted in any form or by any means, electronic or mechanical, including photocopying, recording or any information storage and retrieval system, without either prior permission in writing from the publisher or a licence permitting restricted copying. In the United Kingdom such licences are issued by the Publishers Licensing Society Ltd, 90 Tottenham Court Road, London W1P 9HE.

Scripture quotations unless otherwise noted are from The Holy Bible, New International Version, Copyright © 1973, 1978, 1984 by International Bible Society. Used by permission of Hodder & Stoughton, a Division of Hodder Headline.

Typeset by Arcadia Publishing Services Ltd
Printed and bound in Spain by Bookprint, S.L., Barcelona
ISBN No: 1-904404-05-7

To my dear friends and neighbours
Lucy and Wigbold Van Limburg Stirum
and Silvia Koner,
who with their loyal friendship encouraged me
to bring this work to a successful completion

Contents

November

December

Appendix: Basic Recipes for Stocks, Sauces and Croutons

Preface

Eat soup first and eat it last,
and live till a hundred years be past.
— French Proverb

From antiquity on, soups have always held a very prominent place in the daily fare of monasteries. This is still true today, particularly in French monasteries, where soup is often served twice a day, for the *déjeuner* (lunch) and, even more appropriately, for the *souper*, as the evening meal is called in France. The appeal of soup is universal; it seems to be almost of a basic instinctual nature. Soups are always welcome at any time of the year: hot during the cold weather months and cold during the hot weather. I have always noticed with the guests who arrive at our monastery, how comforted they feel after a bowl of homemade soup is presented to them. It seems an anticipation of the warmth and peace they hope to find during their stay at the monastery.

The soups presented here follow the orderly cycle of the twelve months of the year, with emphasis on produce that is fresh and seasonal and thus available during that specific time of year. This repertoire offers a generous selection of soups per month for those who love to cook and eat a variety of soups, and it will encourage them to continue expanding their experience in the art of soup making.

The soups in this collection range from basic veloutés and consommés to thick and chunky soups, from simple clear broths to creamy soups and more complex potages. I have deliberately simplified the steps in every recipe to the bare essentials (as I do in all my books), so that anyone can easily try them. Throughout the years, many people have told me how they have been discouraged from trying new recipes after encountering so many long and complicated ones.

The recipes contained in this book are meant to help cultivate the art of soup making as well as provide appetizing and nutritious meals. About 75 percent of the recipes are vegetarian, and the rest of them can be easily adapted by vegetarians – for instance, by substituting vegetable stock or bouillon in place of its meat counterpart, or by eliminating the meat or the meat bones in the few places that call for it. Many of these recipes have been created and "re-created" in the kitchen of the monastery of Our Lady of the Resurrection in upstate New York. They are inspired by the simplicity, frugality, and family spirit of the monastic tradition, and they should be enjoyed in the intimacy of the family table. These recipes have nourished, comforted, and satisfied many throughout the years, and they can appeal to the most simple as well as the most refined of palates.

Soup making is an art to be discovered again and again; recipes are to be experimented with, tasted, and then enjoyed. Soup making is basic to life, and thus it is intimately linked to daily living with all that that implies: the rhythm of work and everyday routine, the change of seasons, the size and tastes of families, time limitations, the quality of ordinary meals as well as that of festive celebrations. Soups easily adapt themselves to any situation or circumstance of daily living, and often they bring much comfort to it. As someone once said, soup remains a faithful friend during all of life's occasions. Enjoy, then, the preparation of soups, and extend this joy to your family and friends by sharing the results with them in a warm spirit of conviviality and hospitality. As they say in France, invite them often à la soupe.

As we honour and pay tribute to soup, I also wish to encourage my readers to use the art of soup making to bring relief to the poor and the hungry near or around us. In ancient times, when monasteries were located within the city walls, monks and nuns provided soup and bread to the poor who daily knocked at their doors. Many monasteries still follow this ancient evangelical practice, and this is where the idea of "soup kitchens" to help the poor originated. Places like the Catholic Worker houses in New York City and other American cities daily alleviate the pangs of the hungry and comfort the poor and the weary with a bowl of homemade soup; these soup kitchens rely on the help of volunteers to fulfil their merciful task. Soup making, soup sharing, and soup giving done with love and a selfless spirit can be occasions for endless joy. As the Lord reminds us, whatever we do for the humblest members of his family, we do for him.

Before I put an end to these introductory notes, I wish to thank a long list of people who helped me along the way in the production of this book. First of all, I thank my parents and grandparents, and the many monks who preceded me in the kitchen and from whom I slowly learned the art of soup making. An early and good introduction to this art, as I look back, was very important in the process. Also, many thanks to my agent Howard Sandum, and my editors at Liguori/Triumph (My U.S. publishers), Joan Marlow Golan and Patricia Kossmann, for their encouragement and support. Thanks are also due and given here to the many friends who assisted me in the typing of this manuscript: Anne Poelzl, Eleanor Moorhouse, Jonathan Henry, and Sister J. Regis Catherwood, R.S.H.M., who patiently spent many hours with my scribbles. May the Lord remember them in his kingdom for all their goodness and service provided these past years.

I hope for many years to come you will enjoy with your friends and families the satisfaction that comes from making and sharing soup.

Brother Victor-Antoine d'Avila-Latourrette

Ingredients and Substitutions

The recipes presented here have a kind of universal character, since they spring from many sources and from the four corners of the world. The recipes are purposely written with great simplicity, so that anyone – not just professional cooks – will be encouraged to try them, and thus discover the joys and comforts of making, tasting, and eating soup.

To be truly enjoyed, a good soup needs to be served hot when the recipe calls for hot soup (whenever possible, always serve the hot soups in hot bowls) and cold when the recipe calls for cold soup.

Broth, Stock and Bouillon

Broth – also called stock – is the basis for most soups and they are so much better and richer if the broth or stock is homemade. Not all recipes call for a broths and in some cases the soups create their own broth as they cook. In the Appendix of this book, I present recipes for the basic broths: meat, vegetable, chicken and fish. Broth or stock is very simple to make, but it does take time. When the cook is in a hurry and isn't able to prepare the broth ahead of time, it is perfectly acceptable to use bouillon cubes or canned broth or consommé available from the supermarket. I bring bouillon cubes from France and use them frequently. However, the reader should be aware that some bouillon cubes and canned broths are quite salty, and thus not advisable for those on low-sodium diets. When using bouillon cubes, you might want to omit adding any additional salt for taste.

Some of the recipes here specify a particular flavour of bouillon, which should be respected to give the soup the authentic taste of that recipe. Many other recipes use the generic term "bouillon" in the list of ingredients, and where no flavour is specified, you can choose the flavour of your preference. (Of course, vegetarians can and may always choose vegetable bouillon and achieve great satisfaction in their soups.) Please feel free to experiment with all kinds of bouillon until you discover the one you like best.

Vegetable Broth

A very convenient way to prepare a vegetable broth is to save the water in which vegetables are boiled. Keep saving and adding daily the boiled water from the vegetables you prepare in the course of a week to a container in the refrigerator, and you will have a basic vegetable stock, ready to be used and full of nutrients.

Simmering

"Simmering" is one of the most common words used in soup making. It is an integral part of the process and should not be taken lightly. Simmering has been defined as the quiet, languid movement of the liquids in the soup, which stays at a steady temperature while cooking. The purpose and reason for simmering the soup – that is, cooking it gently and for a long time – is to extract all the best flavours from the ingredients.

Cream Soups and Garnishes

A great number of soups can be made fat free. Cream soups, however, may require for their creaminess the use of milk, heavy cream, yogurt, or sour cream. In most of the recipes here, you can substitute low-fat or skim milk for regular milk, and non-fat yogurt and non-fat sour cream for the regular ones. In some cases, the soup requires heavy cream, and a substitution cannot be made without changing the nature and quality of the soup. In such cases, keep in mind that the fat will be shared by all, and each partaker of the soup will consume only a small amount of fat. If a particular cream soup requires a large number of eggs – say, four – and you are concerned about extra fat and cholesterol, you can cut the number of eggs in half to two, and the soup will still taste fine though less rich. Sour cream may be substituted for crème fraîche as a garnish.

Fat

Most soups require the use of some fat, either oil or butter, in their preparation. In recipes where no particular oil is specified, you can choose your preference. Many cooks, including myself, almost always use olive oil, which is the healthiest, especially for the cholesterol-conscious. (Use extra-virgin olive oil if possible.) Certain regional recipes such as those from Tuscany, Provence, and Spain require olive oil for the authentic flavour, and normally another oil should not be substituted. Similarly, butter gives a distinctive flavour, which is lost if a substitution of another fat is made. Nevertheless, margarine may be used for those who prefer it. Those on low-fat diets may reduce the amount of oil or fat by, say, one third.

Seasonings and Herbs

One of the wonderful things about homemade soups, in contrast to those bought from the supermarket, is that you have complete control over the ingredients that go into the soup, especially the freshness and quality of them. Because so many people, for health reasons, need to limit sodium intake, I recommend that salt be used sparingly. I don't use much salt in my soups, and I often substitute lemon juice and other spices for it. Keep in mind that those who wish more salt in their soups may add it at the table.

Whenever it is possible, fresh-ground pepper should be used according to taste in any recipe that calls for pepper.

Herbs and spices, like salt and pepper, should be used according to taste, and naturally fresh herbs have better flavour than dry ones, especially the dried herbs in the supermarket. Here at the monastery, we have a good herb garden that provides fresh herbs for our table during the growing season. During the cold winter months, we preserve some herb plants in the greenhouse: for example, bay leaf, thyme, rosemary, etc. Other herbs from the garden we dry at harvest time and use in dried form.

4

January

"I give for the month of January,
Courtyards and hall where fires
flame and flare."

– Folgore de San Gimignano

Saint Basil Soup

Ingredients 4–6 servings

6 tablespoons oil of choice
1 large onion, sliced
8 oz, (225g) mushrooms, sliced
2 celery stalks, sliced
2 carrots, sliced

3 pts 8 fl oz, (2 l) water
2 bouillon cubes of choice
salt and pepper to taste
chopped parsley

1. Wash and thinly slice the vegetables.
2. Pour the oil into a soup pot. Add the vegetables and sauté them slightly for 2 or 3 minutes, stirring constantly.
3. Add the water and bouillon cubes. Cook the soup slowly in a covered pot over low heat for 30 minutes. Add salt and pepper and the chopped parsley. Simmer the soup for 10 minutes and serve hot.

This soup is a Western monastic version of a soup that has come down to us from an Orthodox monastery of the Middle East – hence it is named after the great father of Eastern monasticism. Saint Basil the Great (c. 330–379) came from a family remarkable both for wealth and distinction and for holiness – his grandparents, parents, and several siblings were also canonized as saints. During a famine that occurred just before his consecration as bishop of Caesarea in 370, he organized a soup kitchen and personally helped to feed the hungry, as well as donating his inherited wealth to the poor. Saint Basil's Rule is still followed by most Greek Orthodox monks and nuns, and Saint Benedict acknowledged Basil's inspiration in his own Rule.

Chickpea Soup à la Provençale

10 oz, (300g) dried chickpeas
4 fl oz, (120ml) olive oil
4 leeks, white part only, thinly sliced
4 pints 5 fl oz, (2.4 l) water
8 oz, (225g) chopped spinach
4 garlic cloves, minced

4 tablespoons Provencal herbs
 (thyme, rosemary, oregano,
 marjoram, bay leaf)
salt and pepper to taste
1 teaspoon butter or margarine
fried croutons (see recipe p.195)

1. Soak the chickpeas overnight. Rinse them in cold water.
2. Pour the oil into a soup pot, add the thinly sliced leeks, and sauté gently over medium heat for a few minutes. Add the water, chickpeas, spinach, garlic, herbs, and seasonings.
3. Bring the soup to boil, then reduce the heat to low-medium. Cover the pot and cook the soup slowly until the chickpeas are tender (50–60 minutes). Simmer for 15 minutes more.
4. When the soup is done, blend in a blender or food mill. Pour the soup back into the pot and reheat it. Serve the soup in hot bowls. Add butter and a few fried croutons to the top of each serving.

Chickpeas, or *pois chiches*, as they are called in France, have always been a favourite in the Provençal cuisine – or, for that matter, in the cuisine of Mediterranean Europe. The combined flavours of the chickpeas, spinach, and leeks create a marvellous blend. And, of course, the leguminous nature of the chickpea adds an exquisite texture to the soup. To give a true "Provençal" flavour to the soup, be generous in your use of Provençal herbs and use a high-quality extra-virgin olive oil.

Mushroom Soup à la Marie-Louise

Ingredients   *4 servings*

2 celery stalks, including leaves   2 pts, (1.2 l) water (add more if needed)
2 carrots   1 bay leaf
8 ounces (225g) fresh mushrooms   1 bouillon cube
1 large onion   1 teaspoon dried thyme
8 tablespoons oil   salt and pepper to taste

1. Cut the celery, carrots, mushrooms, and onion into thin slices. Mince the onion.
2. Pour the oil into a soup pot and add the onion. Sauté the onion for 1 or 2 minutes, stirring continuously. Add the celery and carrots and continue to stir for another 2 minutes.
3. Pour the water into the pot. Add the mushrooms, bay leaf, bouillon cube, thyme, salt, and pepper. Bring the soup to boil and then let it cook over low heat, covered, for about 40 minutes. Remove the bay leaf and serve the soup hot.

"Soup makes an excellent hot first course. It's simple to prepare and requires very little last-minute attention, yet I have found that it's always greatly appreciated and people think you've gone to a great deal more trouble than you have."
– Rose Elliot, *The Festive Vegetarian*, 1983

Caldo Verde
(Portuguese Cabbage Soup)

Ingredients   *6 servings*

4 fl oz, (120ml) olive oil   3 pts 8 fl oz, (2 l) chicken stock or water
3 onions, chopped   1 cup (8.5 fl oz, 240ml) white wine
6 potatoes, peeled and cubed   salt and pepper to taste
1 small cabbage, chopped

1. Pour the oil into a soup pot and sauté the onions lightly for up to about 5 minutes. Stir often.
2. Add the potatoes, cabbage, chicken stock, wine, salt, and pepper. Bring the soup to boil, then lower the heat and cover the pot. Simmer the soup for about 1 hour. Then turn off the heat and let the soup rest for 10 minutes. Serve hot.

Artichoke and Potato Soup

Ingredients   *6 servings*

4 fl oz, (120ml) olive oil
2 small onions, chopped
2 garlic cloves, minced
17 fl oz, (480ml)
  dry white wine
6 potatoes, peeled and cubed
2 14-ounce jars artichoke hearts
  drained and then chopped

2 tablespoons lemon juice
2.5 pts, (1.4 l) chicken broth
  (or vegetable)
1 bay leaf
salt and pepper to taste
finely chopped parsley as garnish

1. Pour the olive oil into a soup pot and add the onions. Sauté gently over low heat for 2 minutes. Add the garlic and continue sautéing for another minute. Add the wine, cover the pot, and cook over very low heat for 5 more minutes.
2. Add the potatoes, artichokes, and lemon juice. Stir well, cover the pot, and continue cooking over very low heat for another 5 minutes.
3. Add the broth, bay leaf, salt, and pepper. Bring the soup to the boil and stir from time to time. Let it boil for about 5 minutes, then reduce the heat, cover the pot, and simmer for 30 minutes. Remove the bay leaf and serve the soup hot. Garnish with chopped parsley on top of each serving.

Cream of Pea Soup

Ingredients

2 pts, (1.2 l) water
5 oz, (150ml) dried split peas
1 onion, minced
1 carrot, minced
3 tablespoons flour
2 cups milk (17 fl oz, 480ml)
2 egg yolks

1 teaspoon sugar
4 sprigs finely chopped parsley
3 tablespoons oil of choice (or butter or margarine)
3 bouillon cubes
1 bay leaf
salt to taste

1. Pour the water into a soup pot and add the peas, onion, and carrot. Cook, covered, for about 30 minutes over low-medium heat, stirring from time to time. Add the bouillon cubes, bay leaf, salt, sugar, and parsley. Continue cooking over low heat for another 15 minutes.
2. Remove the bay leaf. Mix the oil and flour, making a paste, and then blend this mixture into the soup. Add milk. Stirring continuously, bring the soup to the boiling point and then add the eggs, first mixed in a bowl with a little bit of the soup. Cook for 1 or 2 minutes, stirring constantly, without letting the soup get to the boiling point. Serve hot.

This recipe is but one version of the many varieties of pea soup. Though in my opinion the eggs enhance the taste and smoothness of the soup a great deal, they can be omitted by those who have a cholesterol problem.

Brussels Sprout Soup

16 oz, (450g) Brussels sprouts
3 leeks
8 fl oz, (2 l) water
2 bouillon cubes
4 tablespoons olive oil

3 tablespoons flour
salt and pepper to taste
2 egg yolks
6 slices French bread

1. Cut the Brussels sprouts into thin slices. Slice the leeks and cook them in 1 quart of water for about 5 minutes. Add the bouillon cubes, olive oil, and the other quart of water. Continue cooking for another 40 minutes.
2. In a deep bowl, mix well the flour and 4 tablespoons of soup broth, making a smooth paste. Add this paste to the soup. Add salt and pepper and continue cooking for another 5 minutes. Stir well.
3. Remove the soup from the heat. Beat the egg yolks in 6 spoonfuls of soup broth.
4. Place a slice of bread in the centre of a soup bowl, add 1 teaspoon of the egg mixture on top of the bread, then pour several ladlefuls of the hot soup on top of this. Serve immediately.

This is a very basic recipe that comes to us from the European region encompassing Belgium and northern France, where Brussels sprouts are popular in the local cuisine. The combination of flavours of the leeks and the Brussels sprouts creates a wonderful mild blend that is memorable for days after the soup is tasted. This soup may be prepared exactly as shown in the above recipe, or it may be mixed in a blender with a cup (8.5 fl oz, 240ml) of milk and presented at the table as a creamy potage. Both versions are delicious. The potage variant makes a lovely introductory course to an elegant dinner.

Orzo Soup

4 fl oz, (120ml) olive oil
4 shallots, chopped
1 garlic clove, minced
2 pts, (1.2 l) water or
   vegetable stock
17 fl oz,(480ml) dry white wine
1 bouquet garni (oregano, thyme,
   and bay leaf, tied together and
   removed before serving)

salt and pepper to taste
2 oz, (60g) finely chopped mushrooms
3 oz, (90g) fresh or frozen green peas
4 oz, (100g) orzo noodles
sprinkle dried marjoram (fresh if you have it)
   and grated Romano cheese as garnish

1. Pour the olive oil into a soup pot and gently sauté the shallots and garlic for 1 minute. Stir often.
2. Add the water, wine, bouquet garni, salt and pepper, and bring the mixture to a boil. Lower the heat to moderate and add the mushrooms and peas. Cover the pot and cook the soup for 30 minutes.
3. At this point, add the orzo noodles, check the seasonings, and add more wine if necessary. Simmer the soup, covered, gently for 15 minutes, then remove the bouquet garni and serve the soup hot. Sprinkle marjoram and some Romano cheese on the top of each serving.

"Of soup and love, the first is best."
– Spanish Proverb

Saint Antony Soup

Ingredients   *4–6 servings*

4 tablespoons oil of choice

5 oz, (150g) barley

3 carrots, grated

2 leeks, sliced

1 bay leaf

1¾ oz, (45g) fresh minced parsley or chervil

salt to taste

3 pts, (1.7 l) water

1 bouillon cube and some chopped mushrooms (optional)

1. Pour the oil into a soup pot and add the barley, stirring continuously for 1 minute. Immediately add the carrots, leeks, bay leaf, parsley, salt, and water.
2. Cook the soup over low to medium heat for about 45 minutes, or until the barley is tender. Add more water if necessary. For extra taste, add the bouillon and mushrooms. Serve hot.

Saint Antony of Egypt, called the Great (A.D. 251–356), is considered the father of all monks. He was enormously popular in medieval times as a healer of both men and animals. At age 18, he was so moved by Christ's counsel to "sell all you have, give to the poor, and come follow me" that he did just that. Retiring to the desert as a hermit, he dedicated his life to God in continual prayer, while supporting himself by gardening and mat making. Among the multitudes who consulted Antony for spiritual advice was the emperor Constantine.

Velouté à la Dubarry
(Cauliflower Velouté)

Ingredients   *4 servings*

16 oz, (450g) cauliflower
2 leeks (white part only)
1 potato, peeled
3 pts, (1.7 l) water
4 tablespoons butter
3 tablespoons flour

salt and white pepper to taste
2 egg yolks
8.5 fl oz, (240ml) dry vermouth
2 tablespoons sour cream
pinch of nutmeg

1. Chop the cauliflower and leeks and dice the potato. Place them in a large pot. Add the water and cook slowly, covered, over low-medium heat for 30 minutes.
2. Melt the butter in a separate pot. Gradually add the flour, salt, and pepper and make a roux (thickener), while stirring vigorously. Add some of the broth from the soup and mix well.
3. Place some cooked cauliflower florettes aside, then blend the rest of the vegetable mix in a blender. Return the soup to a clean soup pot. Add the roux, stir, and continue cooking, uncovered, over very low heat, not allowing the soup to reach the boiling point.
4. In a deep bowl, beat the egg yolks. Add the vermouth and sour cream and mix thoroughly. Pour this mixture into the soup. Add the nutmeg and stir well. Check the seasonings. Reheat the soup for a few minutes if it is cold, but again, do not allow it to boil. Serve hot, with the reserved cauliflower on top as garnish.

Cotriade Bretonne

(Fish Soup from Brittany)

8 tablespoons olive oil
3 onions, chopped
6 garlic cloves, chopped and minced
4 pts 5 fl oz, (2.4 l) water
bouquet garni (thyme, bay leaf,
  parsley, and chervil), tied together
  and removed before serving
8 potatoes, sliced in quarters

12 oz, (350g) mackerel (or other fish),
  cleaned and cut in chunks
12 oz, (350g) codfish (or other fish),
  cleaned and cut in chunks
salt and pepper to taste
8.5 fl oz, (240ml) white wine
6 tablespoons chives (or chervil) finely chopped
croutons (see recipe p. 195)

Vinaigrette:
4 fl oz, (120ml) olive oil
4 fl oz, (120ml) balsamic vinegar

salt and pepper to taste
a pinch of dry mustard

1. Pour the olive oil in a soup pot and sauté the onions lightly for 2 or 3 minutes. Add the garlic, water, and bouquet garni, and bring to boil.
2. Add the potatoes, cover the pot, and cook gently for about 30 minutes. Add the fish, salt, pepper, and wine and continue cooking the soup, covered, at a light boil for 15 more minutes.
3. Remove the pot from the heat and pass the soup through a colander. Place the solid parts (fish and potatoes) aside. Ladle the soup bouillon into deep bowls, sprinkle some finely chopped chives on top, add the croutons as garnish, and serve hot.
4. Prepare the vinaigrette by mixing all the ingredients together. Place an equal amount of fish and potato on each plate. Pour the vinaigrette on top and serve immediately after the soup. You may use freshly chopped parsley or chervil as a garnish on top of the vinaigrette.

For a bit of extra taste, add one more cup (8.5 fl oz, 240ml) of dry white wine to the bouillon.

Cherbah

(Arabic Soup)

Ingredients

4 fl oz, (120ml) olive oil
3 onions, sliced
6 tomatoes, peeled and coarsely
  chopped
3 garlic cloves, chopped
1 6-oz (175g) jar red pimientos,
  chopped

1¾ oz, (45g) finely chopped mint
2.5 pts, (1.4 l) stock (vegetable or meat)
4 tablespoons lemon juice
egg yolk, beaten
6 bread slices
salt and pepper to taste

1. Heat the olive oil in a soup pot. Add the onions, tomatoes, and garlic. Sauté for 3 minutes, stirring frequently.
2. Add the pimientos and mint and mix well. Immediately afterward, add the stock (or water and 3 bouillon cubes) and lemon juice and bring to boil. Cover the soup, lower the heat to low-medium, and simmer for 30 minutes.
3. Add the seasonings and blend the beaten egg yolk with 4 tablespoons of the soup. Add this egg mixture to the soup and stir vigorously so it all blends well. Serve the soup hot over 1 slice of bread in the centre of each serving.

Black-Eyed Pea Soup

2 fl oz, (60ml) olive oil
2 onions or leeks, chopped
1 turnip, diced
5oz, (150g) black-eyed peas
  (or one 15-oz can)
6 oz, (180g) rice

salt and pepper to taste
1 bay leaf
6 tablespoons lemon juice (or juice from
  2 lemons)
pinch of cumin
1¼ oz, (30g) fresh parsley, minced

1. Pour the oil into a soup pot and sauté the onions for 2 or 3 minutes, or until they turn golden.
2. Add the turnip, black-eyed peas, broth, rice, salt, pepper, and bay leaf and bring the soup to a boil. Reduce the heat to low-medium, cover the pot, and simmer the soup slowly for 45 minutes, or until the peas are cooked.
3. Add the lemon juice and cumin and stir the soup well. Allow it to sit, covered, for 5 minutes. Remove the bay leaf and serve hot. Sprinkle some fresh parsley on top of each serving.

Spicy English Parsnip Soup

Ingredients

4 parsnips, peeled and sliced
2 medium-sized potatoes,
peeled and cubed
1 large onion, chopped
1 garlic clove, minced
4 tablespoons butter, margarin
  or oil of choice

1 teaspoon curry powder
½ teaspoon ginger powder
2.5 pts, (1.4 l)
  stock of choice
4 fl oz, (120ml) cream
salt and white pepper to taste
chopped parsley, as garnish

1. Melt the butter in a good-sized soup pot and add the prepared vegetables. Sauté them lightly for 2 to 3 minutes.
2. Sprinkle the curry and ginger on top and stir the vegetables thoroughly. Add the stock and bring the soup to boil. Lower the heat and simmer the soup, covered, for 30 minutes.
3. Blend the soup in a blender or food processor until thick and creamy and then return it to the pot. Reheat the soup, add the cream and the seasonings, and stir well. Add more curry if the soup seems to need it. Do not let the soup come to a second boil. Serve the soup hot with some finely chopped parsley as garnish.

The love and taste for parsnips is peculiar to the British Isles and is shared equally by the British and the Irish. Continental Europeans and their South American counterparts regard parsnips as food for cattle and pigs. They may occasionally be used in France in a stew, but rarely. In the United States, parsnips are often used in soups with other vegetables.
I happen to like the individual flavour of parsnips, and I think this soup demonstrates the good use we can make of them.

19

Spinach Cream Soup

Ingredients   *6 servings*

1 package fresh spinach (frozen may
  be substituted)
salt, pepper, and nutmeg to taste
4 tablespoons olive oil
3 pts, (1.7 l) chicken stock (see page 193)

3 eggs
6 tablespoons grated Parmesan cheese
1 onion, sliced
2 garlic cloves, minced
6 slices bread

1. Wash the spinach, making sure it is well cleaned. Then chop it. Chop the onion.
2. Pour the olive oil into a soup pot and briefly sauté the spinach and onion. After 3 minutes, add the chicken stock and cook slowly over low heat for about 30 minutes. Add more stock if necessary
3. Beat the eggs and Parmesan cheese in a deep bowl. Add salt, pepper, and nutmeg and mix it all very well.
4. Blend the soup in a blender until thick and creamy and return it to the pot. Add the egg mixture and stir continually until all the elements blend well. Reheat the soup over low heat for about 5 to 8 minutes.
5. Rub the garlic on the slices of bread and place them in the oven for a few minutes. Place a bread slice in each bowl and immediately pour the hot soup on top. Serve hot.

February

"Come when the rains
Have glazed the snow and clothed the trees with ice,
while the slant sun of February pours
Into the bowers a flood of light."

– William Cullen Bryant

Potage de Navets
(Turnip Soup)

Ingredients   *4 servings*

16oz, (450g) turnips
2 onions or shallots
8 oz, (225g) rice
2.5 pts, (1.4 l) water
17 fl oz, (480ml) milk
  (low-fat can be used)

4 fl oz, (120ml) cream
2 tablespoons butter or margarine
salt and pepper to taste
croutons (optional; see recipe p.195)

1. Slice the turnips in quarters. Place them in the soup pot, add the onions, rice, and water, and boil slowly in a covered pot until vegetables and rice are cooked. Stir from time to time.
2. Take the solid part from the soup, mash it, then put it back into the soup.
3. Add the milk, stirring constantly, while reheating to the boiling point. Add the cream, butter, salt, and pepper and continue stirring for another minute or so. Serve hot. Add a few croutons to each serving as garnish.

"The turnip deserves better treatment than it gets in most kitchens. It is one of our oldest vegetables, cultivated by man for its edible leaves and root for more than 4,000 years. It is popular in France, where it is often part of elegant dishes and cooked in many inventive fashions, yet its versatility is little known or appreciated in the U.S."
  – Bernard Clayton, Jr., *The Complete Book of Soups and Stews*

Saint Scholastica Soup
(Soupe Sainte Scholastique)

Ingredients   *4 servings*

5 pts, (2.8 l) water (more if needed)   2 long carrots, finely chopped
10 tablespoons lentils   2 medium turnips, finely chopped
10 tablespoons split peas   1 celery stalk, finely chopped
8 tablespoons lima beans   1 small head lettuce, finely chopped
2 leeks, finely chopped   3 oz (90g) butter or margarine
4 shallots, finely chopped   salt and pepper to taste

1. Pour water into large soup pot. Add the lentils, split peas, and beans and bring to boil.
2. Add the leeks, shallots, carrots, turnips, and celery stalk. Continue boiling over medium heat in a covered pot for about 30 minutes. Then add the lettuce and simmer for another 30 minutes over a very low heat.
3. Add the butter, salt, and pepper and stir well. Let soup sit, covered, for about 10 to 15 minutes. Serve hot.

Saint Scholastica (d. c. 543) was Saint Benedict's twin, and she was one of the first women to embrace monastic life under the Rule written by her brother. Once a year, she and her brother met halfway between their respective monasteries. On their last visit, after Benedict had resisted his sister's urging to stay and prolong their discussion of the joys of heaven, she prayed for rain to detain him and was answered with a violent thunderstorm. The feast of this revered mother of nuns is celebrated on February 10, and is one of those lovely monastic feasts that brighten our long, dark winters.

French Lentil Soup

6 tablespoons olive oil
1 large onion, chopped
2 garlic cloves, minced
7 oz, (200g) lentils
5 pts, (2.8 l) water
 (more if needed)
1 celery stalk, cut fine
1 turnip, diced

1 bunch sorrel or spinach leaves
1 bay leaf
1 large carrot, finely cut
1 large potato, diced
8.5 fl oz, (240ml) tomato sauce
salt and pepper to taste
2 oz, (60g) cooked rice (optional)

1. Pour the olive oil into the soup pot and gently sauté the onion and garlic for 2 minutes. Stir continually.
2. Wash and rinse the lentils and add them to the soup pot. Add the water, cut vegetables, and the rest of the ingredients except the salt and pepper and rice. Bring to a boil. Then lower the heat to medium and cook slowly, covered, for 1 hour.
3. Add the salt and pepper and let the soup simmer a short while longer. Remove the bay leaf. Serve hot. Add cooked rice if desired.

There are endless varieties of lentil soups. This particular recipe comes to us from France, where two varieties of lentils are grown that can be used for this soup (either the green ones or the dark brown ones). These French lentils are a bit smaller and a bit crunchier than the lentils sold in most supermarkets. This recipe suggests adding rice for the simple reason that the combination of rice and lentils produces the complete protein needed in the daily diet.

Garlic Royale

3 pts 8 fl oz, (2 l) water
  (more if needed)
4 bouillon cubes (or chicken stock
  instead of bouillon and water)
10 garlic cloves, minced
1 bouquet garni (thyme, bay leaf,
  parsley, tied together in cheesecloth)

salt and pepper to taste
dash Tabasco
2 egg yolks beaten
4 fl oz, (120 ml) cream
8.5 fl oz, (240ml) white wine

1. Bring the water to a boil. Add the garlic, bouillon cubes, wine, and bouquet garni. Cover the pot and cook slowly for over 1 hour. Add more water if necessary.
2. Strain the consommé through a thin colander and discard all the solids. Place the consommé back into the pot and add salt, pepper, and Tabasco. Bring to boil and let the soup simmer for 10 minutes.
3. Just before serving, beat the egg yolks and heavy cream. Pour this mixture into the consommé and stir well. Serve immediately

" Surely one of the greatest satisfactions of life is to cook a really delicious meal, a meal that nourishes the body and cheers the spirit, and may be remembered with pleasure for a long time to come."
– Rose Mot, *The Festive Vegetarian*

Polish Pearl Barley Soup

Ingredients   *4–6 servings*

4 tablespoons vegetable oil   3 pts 8 fl oz, (2 l) meat broth (or vegetable)
3 leeks, chopped   8 oz, (225g) barley
2 carrots, peeled and sliced   salt and pepper to taste
1 celery heart, chopped   1¾ oz, (45g) parsley, chopped
1 turnip, diced   sour cream

1. Pour the oil into the saucepan and gently sauté the leeks, carrots, celery, and turnip for about 3 minutes. Stir often.
2. Add the broth, barley, salt, and pepper and bring the soup to boil. Lower the heat, cover the pot, and simmer the soup slowly for 45 to 50 minutes. Add the parsley, stir well, and turn off the heat. Cover the pot and let the soup rest for 10 minutes.
3. Serve the soup hot and place 1 teaspoon sour cream at the centre of each serving.

Quick Black Bean Mexican Soup

Ingredients

4 fl oz, (120ml) olive oil
1 large yellow onion, chopped
4 garlic cloves, minced
1 jalapeño pepper, chopped finely
2 tomatoes, peeled and chopped
2 15-oz cans black beans
2 potatoes, peeled and diced
3 pts, (1.7 l) water

1 bouillon cube
1¾ oz, (45g) fresh corriander, chopped
1 tablespoon cumin
2 tablespoons lime juice
salt and pepper to taste
sour cream as garnish with freshly
chopped corriander all around

1. Pour the olive oil into a good-sized soup pot and sauté the onion for 2 minutes. Add the garlic, jalapeño pepper, and tomatoes, and continue sautéing for another 2 minutes over medium heat, until it turns into a regular sauce. Stir often.

2. Add the beans from their cans with their juice, potatoes, water, and bouillon. Bring the soup to a boil and then reduce the heat to low-medium. Cook slowly, covered, for about 20 minutes.

3. Add the corriander, cumin, lime juice, salt, and pepper. Stir well and continue cooking for another 10 minutes, turn off the heat, and let the soup rest, covered, for 5 minutes. Serve hot and garnish each serving with a teaspoon of sour cream in the centre and freshly chopped corriander around the sour cream.

This is one variation among many traditional Mexican black bean soups. It is a particularly hearty soup with a distinctive flavour of its own because of the jalapeño pepper, cumin, lime juice, and corriander, which are popular spices in Mexican cooking. The sharp, hot flavour of the jalapeño pepper can be reduced by using only half of it, or even omitting it altogether. The garnishes, on the other hand, are very important for the success of this soup, and I recommend strongly that they not be omitted.

Escarole and Bean Minestra

Ingredients   *4–6 servings*

8 tablespoons olive oil
1 large yellow onion, chopped
6 garlic cloves, minced
1 large turnip, diced
4 tomatoes, peeled and chopped
8 oz, (225g) pre-cooked
  white beans or 2 16oz cans
  of the same beans

3 pts, (1.7 l) water
8.5 fl oz, (240ml) white wine
1 medium-sized head escarole, chopped
salt and pepper to taste
grated Parmesan cheese (optional)

1. In a large soup pot, sauté the onion in the oil for a minute or two. Add the minced garlic and mix it well with the onion, stirring often. Add the turnip and tomatoes. Cook the soup over medium heat for 5 minutes, stirring often.
2. Add the precooked beans, water, and wine. Stir the soup and bring it to a boil. Add the escarole and cook the soup over medium heat for about 25 minutes. Add the salt and pepper and simmer for another 10 minutes. Serve hot. You may sprinkle some grated cheese on top.

The slightly bitter–sour flavour of escarole is always welcome, especially as the main ingredient in a traditional Italian soup. Escarole, like many other greens, is extremely rich in vitamins and minerals, and it is readily available in supermarkets all year round. In this particular recipe, the escarole is combined with white beans, producing a wonderfully rich, flavourful soup. For a bit of extra taste, add a bouillon cube – chicken flavour or flavour of choice. One cup (8.5 fl oz, 240ml) of dry white wine also enhances the flavour of the soup.

28

Old-fashioned Cream of Leek Provençal Soup

Ingredients   *6–8 servings*

4 fl oz, (120ml) olive oil
12 leeks (white part only), chopped
3 pts 8 fl oz, (2 l) water
7 oz, (200g) day-old bread
  (more if needed)

3 egg yolks (or at least 2)
7 fl oz, (240ml) milk
salt and pepper to taste
croutons as garnish (see recipe p.195)

1. Sauté the chopped leeks in the oil in a large soup pot over low heat for a few minutes, stirring frequently. (Do not let the leeks turn golden or change colour.) Add the water immediately and bring to boil.
2. Add the day-old. bread. Cover and simmer the soup for 30 minutes, until the leeks are well cooked. Season with salt and pepper. Pass the soup through a sieve or blend in blender. Return the soup to the pot and keep it hot.
3. Break the eggs into a bowl and beat them. Add the milk, salt, and pepper, and blend thoroughly. Add this mixture to the soup, reheat and blend well, and serve it while the soup is hot. Add the croutons on top as garnish.

Bouillabaisse à la Marseillaise

Ingredients

3 fl oz, (80ml) olive oil
2 onions, chopped and minced
4 garlic cloves, minced
3 tomatoes, peeled, seeded, and chopped
1 fennel bulb, finely chopped
6 parsley sprigs, finely chopped
  salt and pepper to taste
3 pts 8 fl oz, (2 l) water
1 bay leaf
3 potatoes, peeled and diced
8 large shrimps
8 scallops or mussels (discard shells)
8 oz, (225g) haddock, cod,
  halibut, monkfish, or rockfish,
  cleaned and cut in small pieces

8.5 fl oz, (240 ml) dry white wine
a good pinch saffron

Sauce Rouille (optional)
4 garlic cloves, peeled and crushed
2 egg yolks
1 tablespoon lemon juice (or dry white wine)
1 tablespoon Dijon mustard
salt and paprika to taste
12.5 fl oz, (360ml) olive oil

1. Heat the oil in a good-sized soup pot. Add the onions, garlic, tomatoes, and fennel. Sauté them lightly over low heat for 2 or 3 minutes.
2. Add the parsley, salt, pepper, water, and bay leaf and bring the soup to a light boil. Simmer the soup for a few minutes, then add the potatoes, scallops, shrimp, cut fish, saffron, and wine. Stir well.
3. Cover the pot and cook the bouillabaisse over high heat for 15 minutes. Then reduce the heat and simmer the soup for another 15 minutes.
4. To make the Rouille or aioli (garlic) sauce, combine all ingredients except the oil in a deep bowl. Mix slowly with an electric mixer. Then, one drop at a time, add the oil until the Rouille thickens to the consistency of mayonnaise. Refrigerate before serving.
5. Ladle into soup bowls as is, or separate the potatoes and the fish, remove the bay leaf, and serve only the broth over slices of French bread covered with a Rouille spread. In that case, serve the potatoes and the fish afterward in a separate dish with more Rouille sauce on the side.

"This bouillabaisse a noble dish is –
A sort of soup, or broth, or brew,
Or hotchpotch of all sorts of fishes,
That Greenwich never could outdo;
Green herbs, red peppers, mussels, saffron,
Sole, onions, garlic, roach, and dace;
All of these you eat at Terré's tavern
In that one dish Bouillabaisse."

– William Makepeace Thackeray,
Ballad of Bouillabaisse

Country Mushroom
and Sour Cream Soup

16 oz, (450g) fresh mushrooms,
  finely chopped
1 bouillon cube
1 large carrot, cut julienne style
1 potato, diced
2 large onions, finely sliced

8 tablespoons olive oil
2.5 pts, (1.4 l) water (more if needed)
salt and paprika to taste
8.5 fl oz, (240ml) sour cream
chopped chives as garnish

1. Prepare the vegetables. Place the oil in a soup pot. Sauté the mushrooms, carrot, potato, and onions for 3 to 4 minutes, stirring continually.
2. Add the water and bouillon cube and cook slowly, covered, over medium heat for 30 to 40 minutes. Add the salt, paprika, and the cup (8.5 fl oz, 240ml) of sour cream. Stir and mix well and simmer for 10 minutes. Serve the soup hot, sprinkling some finely chopped chives on top as garnish.

This is a delicious creamy soup, lavishly enhanced by the thin slices of fresh mushrooms. (Never substitute canned mushrooms for fresh mushrooms, especially in soup, or you will sacrifice flavour and texture.) The sour cream adds an unexpected and inspired touch. This soup must always be served hot.

Soup du Berry

(Red Bean Soup from Berry)

4 fl oz, (120ml) olive oil
3 onions, chopped
10 oz, (300g) precooked
  red beans or the equivalent
  in canned red beans
1 bottle red wine

1 pt 14 fl oz, (960 ml) water or vegetable stock
1 ham bone
1 bay leaf
salt and pepper to taste
¼ teaspoon nutmeg

1. Pour the olive oil into the soup pot and add the onions. Sauté for 2 to 3 minutes. Add the red beans, wine, water, ham bone, and bay leaf. Bring the soup to boil. Then lower the heat to medium-low, cover the pot, and let the soup simmer for 1 hour.
2. Add salt, pepper, and nutmeg. Stir well and continue cooking for another 15 minutes. Turn off the heat and let the soup rest for 10 minutes. Remove the bay leaf and ham bone and serve the soup hot.

Ravioli Potage

Ingredients *4 servings*

3 fl oz, (80ml) olive oil
2 shallots, chopped
salt and pepper to taste
5 oz, (150g) chopped spinach
2 pts, (1.2 l) chicken stock
   (or water and 2 bouillon cubes)

20 oz (600g) fresh or frozen small ravioli
3 tomatoes, peeled, seeded, and chopped
4 sprigs of chervil, chopped
4 teaspoons crème fraîche or sour
cream, as garnish

1. Pour the oil into a good-sized soup pot. Add the shallots and tomatoes. Sauté them gently for 3 minutes.
2. Add the spinach and the stock. Stir and slowly bring the soup to boil. Simmer for about 15 minutes.
3. Add the ravioli, salt, and pepper. Cover the pot and continue simmering for about 8 minutes. Add the chervil, stir, and cover the pot. Turn off the heat and let the soup rest for 5 minutes. Serve the soup hot, and place 1 teaspoon crème fraîche in the centre of each of the soup bowls.

Cheese Velouté

Ingredients   *4 servings*

2 pts, (1.2 l) chicken stock
3 egg yolks
17 fl oz, (480 ml) cream
chervil, finely chopped, as garnish

²/₃ cup grated Gruyère or Parmesan cheese
  or bouillon
10 tablespoons tapioca
salt and pepper to taste

1. Heat the stock and gently bring it to boil. Sprinkle the tapioca gradually into the boiling stock and stir very well. Cook over low-medium heat for about 20 minutes.
2. Place the egg yolks and cream into a deep bowl and mix thoroughly with an electric mixer. Add the cheese slowly and continue to mix to obtain a smooth mixture.
3. Slowly pour the egg-cream mixture into the hot stock. Add salt and pepper. Stir continually and mix very well. Serve the soup hot, sprinkling some finely chopped chervil on top of each serving.

Bulgarian Soup

Ingredients   *6 servings*

3 pts 8 fl oz, (2 l) beef broth
carrots, diced
3 white turnips, diced
1 small celeriac, diced
8 oz, (225g) rice
1 large onion

2 tablespoons butter or margarine
1 teaspoon flour
salt and pepper to taste
2 eggs
4 tablespoons lemon juice
chopped parsley

1. Pour the broth into a large soup pot. Add all the vegetables and rice and cook slowly over medium heat with the pot covered for about 30 minutes.
2. Peel and slice the onion. Melt the butter and sauté the onion briefly, until it begins to turn. Add the flour and mix thoroughly until even.
3. Add the onion mixture and salt and pepper to the soup and continue cooking for 10 minutes.
4. Just before serving, beat the eggs thoroughly with the lemon juice. Add to the soup and stir continually for 1 minute. Serve the soup hot, garnished with finely chopped parsley.

March

"White peason, both good for the pot and the purse,
by sowing too timely, prove often the worse;
Because they be tender, and hateth the cold,
prove March ere ye sow them, for being too bold."

– Thomas Tusser

Saint Lioba Beer and Mushroom Soup

Ingredients   *4–6 servings*

6 tablespoons oil of choice
8 oz, (225g) mushrooms, chopped
2 large onions, chopped
6 cans (3 pts 8 fl oz, 2l) beer
1 bay leaf

2 eggs
4 tablespoons double cream
chopped parsley
salt and pepper to taste
grated Gruyère cheese

1. Pour the oil into a soup pot. Add the mushrooms and onions. Sauté them lightly for a few minutes over low heat. Add the beer and bay leaf and raise the heat to medium. Bring the soup to boil, then simmer slowly for about 20 minutes.
2. In the meantime, in a bowl beat and blend well the eggs and cream. Add 6 tablespoons hot soup to the egg mixture and blend thoroughly.
3. Pour the mixture into the soup, mixing well. Add the chopped parsley, salt, and pepper, and mix well. Reheat the soup over medium heat and continue stirring for a few minutes. Remove the bay leaf and serve the soup hot. Sprinkle some grated cheese on top of each serving.

This German soup is named after Saint Lioba (d. 782), who played a pivotal role in the evangelization of Germany. An Englishwoman, she founded a monastery of nuns in Germany at the request of her cousin Saint Boniface, who later requested she be buried near him. Her monastery became a centre of Christian culture from which abbesses for other houses were taken. Saint Lioba's name means "dear one," and her beauty, intelligence, patience, and loving-kindness endeared her to all who knew her.

Spicy Indian Soup

3 fl oz, (80ml) olive oil
2 onions, chopped
2 garlic cloves, minced
12 oz, (360g) brown or green lentils
3 pts 8 fl oz, (2 l) water
2 carrots, peeled and finely sliced
2 celery sticks, finely sliced

1 teaspoon ground coriander
1 teaspoon cumin
½ teaspoon curry powder
½ teaspoon paprika
6 tablespoons lemon juice
2 teaspoon grated lemon peel
salt and pepper to taste

1. Pour the oil into a large soup pot. Add the onions, garlic, and lentils. Sauté gently over low heat for about 3 minutes. Stir continually and watch that the vegetables don't stick at the bottom of the pot.

2. Pour the water into the mixture, stir, and raise the heat to medium. Bring the soup to boil and add the carrots and celery. Boil for about 20 minutes and then lower the heat to low-medium.

3. Add the coriander, cumin, curry, paprika, lemon juice, lemon peel, salt, and pepper. Stir well and cover the pot. Let the soup simmer gently for about 45 minutes. Check the seasonings and serve hot.

Basic Onion Soup

6 large onions
6 tablespoons olive oil
2.5 pts, (1.4 l) water or stock
4 bouillon cubes (if soup stock is not used)

6 slices bread, toasted
salt and pepper to taste
grated Gruyère cheese

1. Cut the onion into thin slices. Pour the oil into the soup pot and cook the onions slowly until they turn brown. Stir continually.
2. Add the water and bouillon cubes. Bring the water to boil, boil for 5 minutes, and simmer for 10 more. Add the salt and pepper. Stir well.
3. Pour the soup into oven-proof soup bowls. Add a slice of toasted bread on top, cover the entire top of the bowls with grated cheese, and carefully place the bowls into a preheated oven (350°) for 5 to 10 minutes. Serve the soup when the cheese begins to bubble.

French onion soup is probably one of the most popular soups in the world, and there are endless recipes on how to prepare it. The version provided here is one of the easiest. The soup tastes infinitely better with a rich homemade beef or vegetable stock instead of the bouillon cubes. This particular recipe has been reduced to extreme simplicity for the sake of those who lack time to prepare an elaborate soup. For extra flavour and tonic, add to the soup a pinch of cayenne and 4 tablespoons of Calvados liqueur.

Minestrone di Verdura

(Tuscan Green Vegetable Minestrone)

²/₃ cup olive oil
large onion, chopped
2 carrots, sliced
2 celery stalks, sliced
1 15-oz, (450g) can cooked
  cannellini beans
chopped parsley

4 pts 5 fl oz, (2.4 l) water
2 potatoes, peeled and diced
small radicchio, chopped
8.5 fl oz, (240ml) white wine
1 bay leaf
1 15-oz, (450g) can peeled tomatoes
salt and pepper to taste

1. Gently sauté in olive oil the onion, carrots, and celery stalks for about 5 minutes. Add the beans and tomatoes and continue sautéing for 2 more minutes.
2. Add water and bring the soup to boil. Add the diced potatoes, radicchio, wine, bay leaf, parsley, salt, and pepper. Cover the pot and simmer the soup for 60 minutes. Turn off the heat and let the soup stand for 15 minutes. Remove the bay leaf. Serve hot. Grated cheese may be sprinkled on top of each serving.

Everyday Potato Soup

8 potatoes, peeled and diced
3 pts 8 fl oz, (2 l) water or stock
3 onions, sliced
8.5 fl oz, (240ml) milk

salt and pepper to taste
2 tablespoons butter or oil of choice
4 teaspoons chopped parsley (or chervil)

1. Put the potatoes into a soup pot. Add the water and onions and cook over low-medium heat, covered, for about 45 minutes.
2. With a hand masher, mash the potatoes in the soup pot. Add the milk, salt, and pepper and stir the soup, then reheat.
3. Just before serving, add the butter and parsley. Stir and mix well. Serve hot during the cold weather and cold during the warm weather. (When soup is served cold, oil must be used instead of butter.)

This is an easy and economical soup to prepare because all that is needed are some potatoes, a few onions, and a cup (8.5 fl oz, 240ml) of milk. To enhance the soup a bit, add plenty of tender finely chopped fresh parsley. The garnish is a must for a simple soup such as this one.

Garlic Soup

Ingredients

10 large cloves of garlic, well minced
4 fl oz, (120ml) olive oil
3 pts, (1.7 l) water or stock
3 bouillon cubes if stock not used
1 15-oz, (450g) can of tomato sauce

8 slices French bread
1 bay leaf
salt and pepper to taste
2 well-beaten eggs
pinch of cayenne (optional)

1. Sauté garlic in olive oil over low heat without allowing it to brown or burn. Stir continually. Add 3 cups (1 pt 5 fl oz, 720ml) water, bouillon cubes, and tomato sauce. Stir well.
2. Blend the soup in a blender until smooth. Return it to the pot and add remaining water, French bread, bay leaf, salt, and pepper. Bring to a boil, stirring continually, then reduce heat and let cook for about 15 minutes. Then simmer slowly for another 15 minutes. Add cayenne and remove bay leaf.
3. In a deep bowl, beat the 2 eggs gently, adding half a cup (8.5 fl oz, 240ml) of the soup to them and blending the mixture very well. Pour this mixture slowly into the soup, stirring constantly. Simmer for another 5 minutes. Serve hot.

This is a delicious and aromatic soup that is perfectly suited for a cold day in winter. As presented in this recipe, the soup is a popular dish in southern France and northern Spain, where the love of garlic is legendary. Though in the recipe I recommend the use of a blender, a mortar can be used to crush the garlic, as the people of France and Spain still do to this day. And if the tomato sauce (made at home, I hope) remains thick and coarse, so much the better, for it will add texture to the soup.

Lima Bean Soup

Ingredients

4 tablespoons olive oil
1 onion, chopped
3 garlic cloves, minced
3 pts, (1.7 l) water
2 potatoes, sliced in cubes
1 bouillon cube

10 oz, (300g) fresh, dried, or frozen lima beans
parsley, chopped
salt and pepper to taste
1 carrot, sliced
grated cheese of choice as garnish (optional)

1. Pour the oil into a good-sized soup pot. Add the onion and the garlic and sauté lightly for a minute or two over low heat. Stir continually.
2. Add the water, carrot, potatoes, and bouillon cube. Bring to boil over medium heat and then reduce the heat to low.
3. Add the lima beans (less with frozen beans), chopped parsley, salt, and pepper. Cook slowly, over low-medium heat, for about 1 hour, or until the beans are tender. Let the soup sit for 5 minutes, and then serve it hot. Some grated cheese may be sprinkled as garnish on top of each serving.

Béguine Cream Soup

3 pts, (1.7 l) water
2 leeks
4 large potatoes, peeled and diced
4 carrots, peeled and sliced
4 slices stale bread

salt and pepper to taste
½ teaspoon nutmeg
8.5 fl oz, (240ml) single cream
1 tablespoon butter or margarine
chopped parsley and chopped chervil

1. Bring water to boil in a large soup pot. Add the leeks, potatoes, carrots, and bread slices. Lower the heat to moderate, cover the pot, and cook for about 1 hour.
2. Add salt and pepper to taste. Stir the soup. Turn off the soup and let it rest for 5 minutes. Then blend the soup in a food mill or blender till thick and creamy.
3. Return the soup to the pot. Add the nutmeg, cream, and butter. Stir well and bring to a light boil. Add chopped parsley and chervil and serve at once.

This recipe is the version of a soup from Flanders in northern Belgium. Its name suggests it originated among the Béguines. Béguinage was a medieval institution that allowed pious laywomen to lead a form of religious life in common, without becoming actual nuns. It was one of the few alternatives to either marriage or the cloister. The Béguines lived in beautiful small houses attached to each other. They were independent and were allowed to keep their servants. However, they had a common church for their devotions, and they had each other for mutual company. In general, they were a progressive group of women who wished to assert, as much as the times allowed, their independence from men. They were women of great culture, and some of them became renowned mystics. The Béguines, as an institution, flourished particularly in Holland and the Flemish section of Belgium.

Bread and Milk Soup

Ingredients   *4 servings*

4 tablespoons butter or margarine   4 slices bread cut into quarters
4 tablespoons flour   salt and pepper to taste
1 pt 14 fl oz, (1 l) milk   1 beaten egg
  (more if necessary)   1¾ oz, (45g) chopped parsley or chervil
1 onion, chopped and minced

1. Melt the butter in a soup pot. Add the flour and half a cup of milk, stirring all the time.
2. Add the onion and the rest of the milk. Bring the soup to boil. Add the bread and seasonings and simmer the soup for 10 to 15 minutes. Stir occasionally.
3. When the soup is done, add the beaten egg and blend thoroughly. Sprinkle the fresh chopped parsley on top of the soup. Serve hot.

"Soup as a main course,
soup to begin the meal,
and when it is homemade,
it is soup to nourish the soul."
— Julia Child, *The French Chef Cookbook*

Fava Bean Soup

Ingredients   *4 servings*

2 onions, chopped fine

3 fl oz, (80ml) olive oil

1 15-oz, (450g) can fava beans
  (or the equivalent in dried ones
  soaked overnight and rinsed
  twice in fresh water)

1 carrot, diced

1 large potato, peeled and diced

3 oz, (90g) fresh or frozen peas

1 small branch thyme
  (or 1 teaspoon dried thyme)

1 ham bone (or 1 slice ham thinly cut)

3 fl oz, (80ml) sherry

salt and cayenne pepper to taste

croutons (optional; see recipe p.195)

2.5 pts, (1.4 l) water

1. Place the onions in the soup pot and sauté them in olive oil for about 2 minutes.
   Stir frequently.
2. Add the fava beans (without their juice), carrot, and potato. Stir well and add the water.
   Over medium heat, bring the water to boil.
3. When the water is boiling, add the peas, thyme, and ham bone and cover the pot.
   Cook slowly over low-medium heat for 30 minutes.
4. Add the sherry, salt, and cayenne pepper (just a dash). Stir well, cover the pot, and
   simmer for another 15 minutes. Remove the ham bone and the thyme. Add the croutons
   on top of each serving as garnish.

Watercress Soup

Ingredients   *4–6 servings*

4 tablespoons butter, margarine, or oil of choice
4 leeks, chopped
1 bunch fresh watercress, chopped
4 potatoes, peeled and cubed
2 pts, (1.2 l) water (or stock)
1 bouillon cube (if water is used
  instead of stock)

13 fl oz, (360ml) milk (for richer
  soup, use 8.5 fl oz, (240ml)
  cream instead)
salt and pepper to taste
1 egg yolk, beaten (optional)
6 tablespoons crème fraîche,
  as garnish
chopped chervil, as garnish

1. Melt the butter or oil in a large soup pot. Add the leeks and watercress and sauté them gently for 2 to 3 minutes.
2. Add the potatoes and continue sautéing for 1 minute extra, stirring frequently. Add the water or stock and the bouillon cube (if necessary). Bring the soup to boil, and then cover the pot. Simmer the soup gently for 30 minutes.
3. Blend the soup in a blender and return it to the pot. Add milk and simmer for another 10 minutes. (At this point, if you wish, add the egg yolk and mix thoroughly.)
4. Serve the soup in well-heated bowls. Place 1 teaspoon of crème fraîche in the centre of each serving and sprinkle the chopped chervil all around it.

Saint Patrick Irish Cheddar Soup

Ingredients   *4–6 servings*

2 leeks
2 potatoes
4 carrots
4 tablespoons butter or margarine
2.5 pts, (1.4 l) vegetable or
   meat stock

¼ teaspoon sage powder
salt and pepper to taste
8.5 fl oz, (240ml) milk
5 oz, (150g) grated mild cheddar cheese
1 garlic clove, minced
¼ teaspoon thyme powder

1. Clean, peel, and chop the vegetables. Melt the butter in a soup pot and sauté the vegetables lightly for about 3 minutes. Stir frequently.
2. Add the stock, garlic, herbs, and seasonings. Bring the soup to boil, then cover the pot and let it simmer for 30 minutes.
3. Blend the soup in a blender and return it to the pot. Add the milk and cheese. Reheat the soup, but do not allow it to boil again. Serve hot.

Harrira

(Moroccan Bean Soup)

2 oz, (60g) chickpeas, soaked overnight
2 oz, (60g) lima beans
2 oz, (60g) black beans, soaked overnight
2 oz, (60g) red kidney beans,
  soaked overnight
2 oz, (60g) lentils
2 oz, (60g) split peas (yellow, if possible)
2 oz, (60g) navy beans, soaked overnight
5 pts, (2.8 l) water (more as needed)
2 large onions, chopped

1 16-oz can tomatoes, chopped
½ teaspoon each, ginger, turmeric,
  cumin, cinnamon
¼ teaspoon black pepper
1 tablespoon lemon juice
2 tablespoons flour
1 bunch fresh corriander, chopped
8 leaves of fresh mint, chopped
salt to taste
pinch of cayenne
a good pinch of paprika

1. Place all the beans in a large pot, add the water, and bring to boil. Simmer for 1½ hours.
2. Add the onions, tomatoes with their juice, ginger, turmeric, cumin, cinnamon, black pepper, and lemon juice. Stir well, cover the pot, and bring the soup to a second boil. Reduce the heat to low-medium and simmer the soup for another hour.
3. Add the salt and more water if necessary. Dissolve the flour in a quarter cup of cold water and make a paste. Add a few tablespoons of the hot soup, mix thoroughly, and pour into the soup. Stir vigorously and continually so that the soup gradually thickens but without any lumps.
4. Add the corriander (or parsley) and mint, cayenne powder, and paprika. Stir well and cook over low heat for 15 to 20 minutes. Serve hot.

This is the original fragrant soup from ancient Morocco. There, it is traditionally served during the 30-day Ramadan fast just before sunset, when the daily fast is broken, to strengthen the faster for the next day's fast.

Butternut Squash Soup Portuguese Style

Ingredients   *6 servings*

6 tablespoons olive oil
3 onions, chopped
5 garlic cloves, minced
2 butternut squash, peeled, halved, seeded, and cut in chunks
1 potato, peeled and cubed

1 carrot, peeled and sliced
3 pts, (1.7 l) vegetable or chicken stock
salt and pepper to taste
1¼oz, (30g) freshly minced parsley
fresh thyme leaves as garnish

1. Pour the olive oil into a large soup pot and sauté the onions and garlic over low heat for 3 to 5 minutes. Turn off the heat, cover the pot, and let the onion-garlic mixture steam for 15 minutes.
2. Add the squash, potato, and carrot and stir the mixture well. Pour the stock and bring the soup to boil. Reduce the heat, cover the pot, and let it simmer for 45 minutes.
3. Add the seasonings and parsley, stir well, cover the pot, and continue simmering for another 15 minutes.
4. Blend one third of the soup at a time in a blender or food processor and return it to the original but clean pot. Reheat the soup over low heat, but do not let it come to boil. Serve hot and sprinkle fresh thyme leaves on top of each serving as garnish.

Soup Julienne

Ingredients   *6 servings*

3 leeks (white part only)
3 carrots
3 medium-sized turnips
½ medium-sized head cabbage, shredded
1 onion

5 pts, (2.8 l) water or vegetable
  or chicken stock
3 bouillon cubes of choice
  (if stock is not used)
salt and pepper to taste
1¼ oz, (30g) minced parsley

1. Wash and rinse the vegetables. Slice them julienne style. Place them in a good-sized soup pot and add the water. Add the bouillon cubes and bring the water to boil. Reduce the heat to medium, cover the pot, and cook the soup slowly for about 60 minutes, stirring from time to time.

2. When the soup is done add salt, pepper, and parsley, and stir a few times then cover the pot and simmer for 5 minutes more. Serve hot.

April

"'Sing a song of Spring,' cried the pleasant April rain
With a thousand sparkling tones upon the window pane,
And the flowers hidden in the ground woke dreamily and stirred,
From root to root, from seed to seed, crept swiftly the happy word."

– Celia Thaxter

Cream of Mushroom Soup à la Romaine

Ingredients   *4 servings*

4 tablespoons butter or margarine
8 oz, (225g) chopped mushrooms
1 onion, chopped
1 carrot, sliced
2 garlic cloves, minced
pinch of thyme

2 tablespoons flour
1 pt 14 fl oz, (1 l) water
salt and pepper to taste
17 fl oz, (480ml) cream
grated Romano cheese

1. Melt the butter in a soup pot. Add the mushrooms, onion, carrot, garlic, and thyme. Cover the pot and let the vegetables simmer for 5 minutes over very low heat.
2. Add the flour and stir well. Add the water, stir some more, and bring the soup to a quick boil. Over low heat, simmer for 30 minutes.
3. Blend the soup in the blender and then return it to the soup pot. Add the seasonings and cream and mix well. Reheat the soup, but do not let it boil again. Serve the soup hot and sprinkle grated Romano cheese on top of each bowl.

"Mushrooms of one night be the best
and they be little and red within
and closed at the top;
and they must be peeled
and then washed in hot water
and then parboiled
and if you wish to put them in a pasty
add oil, cheese, and spice powder."
— The Goodman of Paris (*Le Ménagier de Paris*)

54

Sweet Milk Soup for Children

Ingredients   *4 servings*

17 fl oz, (480ml) water
7 oz, (200g) bread cubes
17 fl oz, (480ml) milk
1¾ oz, (45g) raisins

4 tablespoons real maple syrup
2 beaten eggs
dash nutmeg

1. Pour the water into the soup pot, add the bread, and bring to boil, then simmer for 10 minutes.
2. Add the milk, raisins, and maple syrup. Stir well and bring the soup to a second boil. Add the beaten eggs and nutmeg. Blend well and simmer for 10 more minutes before serving.

This soup is a simple concoction that children have enjoyed throughout the ages. It has been prepared and served by mothers in a thousand different ways – e.g., using wild honey instead of syrup or berries instead of raisins. It has always lived up to young children's expectations and filled their hearts with utter delight.

Potage Villageois

(Village Vegetable-Macaroni Soup)

Ingredients   *6 servings*

3 leeks   5 oz, (150g) small macaroni noodles
4 tablespoons butter or margarine   17 fl oz, (480ml) milk
1 small cabbage   salt and pepper to taste
2.5 pts, (1.4 l) water   minced parsley
1 bouillon cube   grated Parmesan cheese
6 potatoes, cubed

1. Slice the leeks and cabbage julienne style and sauté them in butter for a few minutes over low heat.
2. Add the water and bouillon cube. Add the cubed potatoes. Bring the water to boil and cook over medium heat for 30 minutes.
3. While the soup is boiling, cook the macaroni in a separate pot. When it is cooked, drain.
4. Add to the soup the cooked macaroni, milk, salt, pepper, and minced parsley. Allow the soup to come to boil and then turn down the heat. Keep the cover on the pot and allow the soup to simmer for a few minutes. Serve the soup hot and garnish it at the last minute with grated Parmesan cheese.

This is a typical soup often served in the evening throughout the old villages of France – hence the name. It is a French version of the Italian minestrone, and other vegetables, like carrots or beans, may be added to it. Very often the French prefer the use of spaghetti-type noodles instead of macaroni for the preparation of this soup. If you decide to use spaghetti, break the noodles in half for easier eating.

Borscht

Ingredients   *8 servings*

2 red beets
2 carrots
2 potatoes
2 leeks
½ head red cabbage
10 mushrooms
finely minced parsley

2 tomatoes
6 pts, (3.3 l) water
4 tablespoons olive oil
salt and pepper
double cream or sour cream (1 tablespoon per serving)
1 onion

1. Wash and peel the beets, carrots, and potatoes. Dice them into small cubes.
   Cut the leeks, cabbage, mushrooms, onion, and tomatoes into small pieces.
2. In a large soup pot, bring water to boil, then add the oil and all the vegetables.
   Cover and cook over low-medium heat for about 30 minutes. Add salt and pepper to the
   soup and stir. Let the soup sit for 15 minutes, covered.
3. Reheat the soup for a few minutes and serve hot, adding 1 tablespoon of heavy cream
   and some minced parsley to the centre of each serving.

Sour Cream Soup

Ingredients   *4–6 servings*

6 medium potatoes, peeled
2.5 pts, (1.4 l) water
3 large bay leaves
1½ tablespoons caraway seeds (or to taste)
salt to taste

¹/₈ cup flour (or more if necessary)
4 fl oz, (120ml) milk
17 fl oz, (480ml) sour cream
 (more if needed)
chopped scallions as garnish

1. Dice the potatoes very small and put them into the soup pot with the water.
    Add the bay leaves, caraway seeds, and salt. Cook until the potatoes are done.
    Do not drain the water.
2. Stir the flour into the milk and make a paste. Pour this mixture into the soup, stirring
    constantly while adding. This will thicken the soup.
3. Add the sour cream to the soup, stirring constantly while adding. Let the soup again
    come to the boil and then simmer it slowly for about 10 minutes. Remove the bay
    leaves and serve hot or cold. Add some chopped scallions as garnish on top of each
    serving.

"You must observe in all broths and soups that one thing does not taste more than another; but that the taste be equal, and it has a fine agreeable relish, according to what you design it for; and you must be sure that all greens and herbs you put in be cleaned, washed and picked."
– Hanna Glasse, *The Art of Cookery*, 1776

Potage Germiny

(Sorrel Soup)

Ingredients   *6 servings*

3 pts 8 fl oz, (2 l) chicken or beef stock
4 tablespoons butter or margarine
1 lb, (450g) thinly chopped and shredded
  sorrel leaves (about 20 leaves)
salt and pepper to taste

4 tablespoons finely chopped chervil
3 egg yolks
8.5 fl oz, (240ml)
single cream

1. Place the stock in a large soup pot and cook over low-medium heat. Reduce heat gradually.
2. Melt the butter in a separate pot and add the chopped sorrel. Cook over low heat until the sorrel is tender and turns into a sauce. Add the chervil, blend well, and turn off the heat.
3. Place the egg yolks and cream in a deep bowl and mix them well. Pour this mixture into the soup stock and mix it well. Do not let it reach the boiling point.
4. Add the sorrel-chervil mixture and also the seasonings to the soup. Stir and mix well. Serve hot or refrigerate and serve cold, depending on the season.

Cream of Curry Potage

6 tablespoons crème fraîche
2 tablespoons curry powder
4 egg yolks
1 lemon

2.5 pts, (1.4 l) chicken (or vegetable) stock
salt to taste
croutons as garnish (see recipe p.195)

1. In a large, deep bowl, place the crème fraîche, curry, egg yolks, and juice from the lemon. Mix thoroughly with an electric mixer.
2. Put the stock in a soup pot and bring it to boil. Fill one cup with the stock and pour it over the egg-curry mixture. Mix well.
3. Pour the contents of the bowl into the boiling stock and continue to boil for 3 to 4 minutes, stirring constantly.
4. Place 4 croutons in each soup plate or bowl. Pour the soup over them and serve at once.

"Soup is a mainstay of civilization. It is a creative synthesis of flavours and textures, served in a comforting, back to childhood style; or as a precise and perfectly elegant beginning to the shape of things to come."

– Liz Smith

Shrimp Soup de Luxe

Ingredients *4 servings*

4 tablespoons olive oil
2 onions, minced
8 oz, (225g) tiny fresh
  or frozen shrimps
8.5 fl oz, (240ml)
  dry white wine
8.5 fl oz, (240ml) water

1 pt 5 fl oz, (720ml) milk (low fat can be used)
½ teaspoon dry mustard
3.5 oz, (90g) fresh chopped herbs: dill,
  chives, tarragon, and parsley
salt and white pepper to taste
sour cream as garnish

1. Heat the olive oil in a soup pot. Add the onions and shrimp. Cook and stir continually for about 5 minutes until both the shrimp and the onions look soft and tender.
2. Add the wine, water, and mustard and bring the soup to boil. Lower the heat to medium and continue cooking for another 10 to 15 minutes.
3. Add the milk and seasonings and continue to cook the soup slowly for another 15 minutes. Stir often. Just before serving, add the cup of chopped herbs, mix well, and then ladle the soup into soup plates or bowls. Garnish with a teaspoon of sour cream on top of each serving.

A dear friend of mine who shared this recipe with me assures me that every time he serves this soup he gets wonderful compliments from his guests. The soup captures the rich, sweet taste of the shrimp, which are well complemented by the taste of the fresh herbs. This soup makes an ideal first course to an elegant dinner.

Three Peppers Soup

Ingredients   *4 servings*

3 peppers, 1 red, 1 yellow, and 1 green
4 garlic cloves
5 teaspoon olive oil
2 pts, (1.2 l) beef or
    vegetable stock (or water
    and 3 bouillon cubes)

½ teaspoon saffron
8 slices bread (2 for each person)
4 eggs
salt and white pepper to taste
paprika as garnish

1. Roast the peppers for 30 minutes. Let them cool and then peel them. Cut them in long, thin strips. Peel and chop garlic cloves.
2. Heat the oil in a soup pot and add the peppers and garlic. Cook for 1 minute, stirring continually. Add the stock and the saffron, stir some more, cover the pot, and cook over moderate heat for about 30 minutes.
3. Toast the bread slices and place them on a plate. Break the eggs and place them individually one by one into the soup. (Do this carefully so as to keep them whole.) Add salt and pepper if desired.
4. Turn off the heat. Cover the pot and let the soup rest for 5 minutes, until the egg whites are cooked. Carefully place 2 slices of bread into each soup bowl, place 1 egg on top, and then cover them with the rest of the soup. Sprinkle some paprika on top and serve immediately.

"I regard cold hors d'oeuvres as quite unnecessary in a dinner;
I even consider them counter to the dictates of common sense,
and they are certainly injurious to the flavour of the soup that
follows."

– August Escoffier

Cream of Asparagus Soup

3 pts 8 fl oz, (2 l) water

8 oz, (225g) asparagus, tough ends removed, cut into 1-inch lengths

1 potato, peeled and diced

1 onion, sliced

1 medium carrot, sliced

8.5 fl oz, (240ml) double cream

2 tablespoons butter or margarine

salt and pepper to taste

1. Cook the vegetables in the boiling, salted water until they are tender. Pass the soup through a sieve or blend in a blender.

2. Return the soup to the pot, add the heavy cream, butter, salt, and pepper and stir, bringing the soup to boil. Stir again. Cover the pot and let the soup simmer for another 10 minutes. Serve hot.

If one wishes the soup to be of a thicker consistency, one can easily substitute 2 cups (17 fl oz, 480ml) of white sauce (see recipe p. 194) for the cream.

Saint Joseph Chickpea Soup

Ingredients

10 oz, (300g) chickpeas
4 pts 5 fl oz, (2.4 l) water
10 oz, (300g) canned tomatoes
1 large onion, chopped
1 stalk celery, minced
2 carrots, sliced

4 cloves of garlic, minced
1 red pepper, diced
4 tablespoons olive oil
1 bouillon cube
1 bay leaf
salt and pepper to taste

1. Soak chickpeas overnight. Boil them in plenty of water, add all the remaining ingredients, and cook slowly over medium heat for about 1 hour, until the peas and all the vegetables are tender.

2. Add salt and pepper. Simmer the soup, covered, for about 15 minutes. Remove the bay leaf before serving. Serve hot.

Saint Joseph, Jesus' foster father, is the patron of fathers of families, bursars and procurators, manual workers, especially carpenters, the Universal Church, and those who pray for a holy death. Always honoured by followers of the monastic path, including Saint Teresa of Avila, he is the saint to whom monks and nuns make recourse whenever there is a serious financial problem in a monastery. His feast is celebrated on March 19, and he has an additional feast day on May 1, as Saint Joseph the Worker.

Cuban Black Bean Soup

Ingredients

16 oz, (450g) dried black beans
5 pts, (2.8 l) water
4 fl oz, (120ml) olive oil
3 onions, chopped
1 bell pepper, chopped
6 garlic cloves, minced
1 teaspoon thyme

½ teaspoon oregano
1 bay leaf
3 teaspoons sugar
4 teaspoons vinegar
salt and pepper to taste
pinch of cumin

1. Soak the beans overnight. Rinse the beans and discard the water. Place the beans and 12 cups (5 pints, 2.8 litres) of water in a large soup pot. Bring the water to boil, lower the heat, cover the pot, and cook the beans slowly for 1 hour or until the beans are tender.
2. Pour the oil into a separate pot, add the onions, pepper, and garlic cloves, and sauté them lightly for about 2 to 3 minutes.
3. Take out 1 cup of cooked beans from the large pot and purée them in a blender. Add the purée to the sautéed vegetables and mix well. Add the whole mixture to the rest of the beans in the soup pot.
4. Add the thyme, oregano, bay leaf, sugar, vinegar, salt, pepper, and cumin. Stir well, cover the pot, and simmer for about 45 to 50 minutes. Remove the bay leaf and let the soup stand, covered, for another 10 minutes. Serve hot.

Vermicelli Soup

Ingredients   *6 servings*

4 pts 4 fl oz, (2.4 l) water   3 oz, (90g) vermicelli noodes
4 vegetable bouillon cubes   1¾ oz, (45g) fresh parsley, minced
3 garlic cloves, minced   salt to taste
1 onion, thinly sliced and minced   grated cheese of choice
2 carrots, cut in small cubes

1. Pour the water into a soup pot and bring it to boil. Add the bouillon, garlic, and the cut-up the vegetables and cook them for about 25 minutes. Add the vermicelli noodles and continue cooking for another 10 minutes over medium heat.
2. Add the minced parsley and salt. Cover the pot and simmer the soup for 5 more minutes before serving. Sprinkle grated cheese on the top of each soup plate or bowl just before serving. Serve hot.

Brussels Sprout Cream Potage

Ingredients

2 tablespoons butter or margarine
16 oz, (450g) Brussels sprouts,
  sliced into quarters
16 oz, (450g) potatoes, peeled and diced
2 leeks or onions, sliced
3 garlic cloves, minced

3 pts 8 fl oz, (2 l) water
pinch of thyme
salt and pepper to taste
1 bay leaf
17 fl oz, (480ml) milk

1. Melt the butter in a saucepan and sauté the Brussels sprouts, potatoes, onions, and minced garlic for 1 or 2 minutes. Stir continuously. Add the water and seasonings and cook slowly over low-medium heat for 40 to 45 minutes, or until soup is done. Remove the bay leaf.
2. Cook separately from the above some Brussels sprouts sliced into 4 even quarters, to be used as garnish on top of the soup.
3. When the soup is done, add the milk and stir well. Blend the soup in a blender and serve hot. Garnish each serving with the Brussels sprouts.

May

"Upon the first of May,
With garlands fresh and gay,
With mirth and music sweet,
For such a season meet,
They passe their time away"
　　　　– 16th-century Old English song

Russian Chtchavel

12 oz sorrel (20 leaves)
3 pts 8 fl oz, (2 l) water
2 garlic cloves
3 hard-boiled eggs
black bread cut into cubes

½ pint double cream
salt to taste
1 cucumber, thinly sliced (fresh or pickled)
the juice of 1 lemon

1. Chop the sorrel and put it in a soup pot. Add the water and bring to boil. Lower the heat to low-medium and cook for 20 minutes.
2. While the sorrel is cooking, chop the garlic and hard-boiled eggs. Add the garlic, eggs, and juice of the lemon to the soup. Continue cooking for 15 minutes.
3. Just before serving, add the cream, salt, and cucumber. Stir well.
4. Place the bread cubes in the soup bowls and pour the soup over the bread. Serve hot.

*R*ussian cookery is known for its abundance of soups. The long and severe winters make it imperative for the Russian people to think of heartwarming soups using every kind of produce available. Throughout the centuries, they have used their imagination and industriousness to test and discover suitable ways to use fresh, pickled, spicy, cured, or dry vegetables, as well as fruits, berries, mushrooms, meat, bread, and dairy products in their soups. Chtchavel is an example of the resourcefulness of the Russians in soup making.

Potage Clamart
(Turnip-Leek Potage)

Ingredients   *4 servings*

6 tablespoons oil of choice or butter
  or margarine
3 oz, (75g) fresh peas
1 carrot
1 turnip
2 leeks

1 pt 14 fl oz, (1 l) water
salt to taste
thyme and rosemary to taste
1 egg yolk
2 teaspoons double cream

1. Wash and rinse vegetables. Cut carrot, turnip, and leeks in thin slices.
2. Pour the oil into the soup pot and add the peas, carrot, turnip, and leeks.
    Cook slowly over very low heat for 2 minutes. Stir continually.
3. Add water, pinch of salt, thyme, and rosemary. Cook the soup slowly, keeping it
    covered for 30 minutes. Turn off the heat and let the soup stand for 15 minutes.
4. Blend the soup in a blender or put it through a sieve and return it to the pot. Add the
    beaten egg yolk and heavy cream and stir well. Serve hot.

*This potage originated in Clamart, which is one of the neighbouring
suburbs just outside the city of Paris. It is a very tasty potage,
due in great part to the special flavour given by the fresh peas. Ideally,
this soup should be prepared in early spring when the fresh peas are in
season, or later in the autumn, when fresh peas are again harvested.
The beaten egg and the cream enhance the creamy nature of the soup.
If the potage is being prepared for an elegant dinner party, it should be
garnished with some finely chopped chervil or hard-boiled eggs, as a
finishing touch.*

Shaker-Style Soup

Ingredients   *4 servings*

2 tablespoons butter or margarine

2 tablespoons flour

2 6-oz, (175g) cans tomato paste

1 onion, chopped and minced

4 teaspoons dill

salt and pepper to taste

1 pt, (600ml) water

1 pt, (600ml) milk

4 fl oz, (120ml) sour cream

1. Melt the butter or margarine in a soup pot. Add the flour. Stir and mix well. Add the tomato paste, chopped onion, dill, salt, pepper, and water. Stir constantly and bring to boil, then simmer for 20 minutes.
2. Heat the milk separately, add the sour cream to the hot milk, and mix well. Pour the milk-cream mixture into the soup and blend well. Use fresh chopped dill as garnish on top of each serving and serve hot.

"Shaker cookery, like everything Shaker designed or Shaker created, is traditionally simple and functional. If it is gourmet gastronomy you seek, or some rare epicurean dainty, forget it. You won't find exotics among these recipes. What you will find are simple directions for the preparation of tested comestibles, each conceived with loving care, to be of delicious taste and a wholesome, satisfying nature. When you get right down to it, isn't that what good food is all about? The Shakers, bless them, have known it for over a hundred years."

– Martin Dibner

Asparagus–Orange Velouté

Ingredients   *4 servings*

16 oz, (450g) asparagus,
  peeled and well washed
1 pt 14 fl oz, (960ml) water
1 teaspoon sugar
4 fl oz, (120ml) freshly squeezed
  orange juice
2 egg yolks

8.5 fl oz, (240ml) dry white wine
2 tablespoons crème fraîche (or sour cream)
4 tablespoons butter or margarine
3 tablespoons flour
salt and white pepper
pinch nutmeg

1. Peel the hard part of the asparagus and wash it well. Place the asparagus in a soup pot, add water, and cook at a gentle boil for 20 minutes. Drain the asparagus and preserve the water. Cut the asparagus stalks in half and place the top portions aside.
2. Melt the butter or margarine in another pot, add the flour a little at a time, and stir continuously. Add the water from the asparagus, the asparagus bottoms, salt, and pepper, and cook for 5 or 6 minutes, stirring continuously.
3. Blend the soup in a blender and return it to the soup pot. Continue cooking it over very low heat, not allowing the soup to come to a boiling point.
4. Beat the egg yolks in a deep bowl, add the wine, crème fraîche, and sugar and mix thoroughly. Pour this mixture into the soup. Add the orange juice, nutmeg, and asparagus tops and check the seasonings. Stir well and reheat the soup for a few minutes until it is hot. Don't let it boil. Serve immediately.

*T*his is a light, tasty, and elegant velouté, to be served during an intimate dinner party. It is particularly attractive in early spring, when asparagus is in season. The orange juice blends wonderfully with the taste of the fresh asparagus.

Cabbage Soup

5 pts, (2.8 l) water   1 bouillon cube
1 head cabbage   1 teaspoon each parsley, thyme, and marjoram to taste
3 leeks or onions   2 celery stalks
salt and pepper to taste   2 medium potatoes

1. Place the water in a large soup pot. Shred the cabbage and slice the leeks and celery. Add them to the water.
2. Peel and dice the potatoes. Add the potatoes and bouillon cube to the soup. Cover the pot and allow the soup to cook slowly over low-medium heat for at least 2 hours. Add more water if necessary.
3. When the soup is done, add the parsley, thyme, marjoram, salt, and pepper. Cover the pot and let the soup stand for 30 minutes before serving.

Cabbage is one of the most utilized vegetables in both northern Europe and America. In France it is also popular, especially in the northeastern corner of the country, near the German and Belgian borders. This classic soup probably originated in that area. It is hearty and filling and can be used as a complete meal. It is particularly appetizing on a cold winter night.

74

Potage Céline

(Carrot-Celeriac Soup)

Ingredients   *6–8 servings*

4 oz butter or margarine (or oil   1 onion
of choice)   3 pts 8 fl oz, (2 l) water
16 oz, (450g) carrots   salt and pepper to taste
8 oz, (225g) celeriac   chervil (or parsley), well chopped

1. Melt the butter in a soup pot. Add carrots, celeriac, and onion sliced very thin or cut julienne style. Sauté vegetables for a few minutes and then add water.
2. Cook for a half hour, then add the salt and pepper according to taste. Stir well.
3. Blend the soup in a blender, then put it back into the pot and continue to cook slowly over low heat for about 15 to 20 minutes. Simmer a few minutes more.
4. Just before serving, add the chopped chervil and mix well. Serve hot, or chill for about 2 hours and serve cold. If soup is to be served cold, use oil instead of butter.

Cream of Broccoli Soup

Ingredients

16 oz, (450g) fresh broccoli
3 medium-sized potatoes
2 onions
pinch of cayenne
grated cheese of choice as garnish

8.5 fl oz, (240ml) double cream (or cream
  and milk for lighter option)
salt to taste
3 pts 8 fl oz, (2 l) water
1 bouillon cube

1. Wash, peel, and slice the vegetables into small pieces. Pour the water into a large soup pot and add all the vegetables and the bouillon. Cook slowly over medium heat for 1 hour.
2. Blend the soup in a blender and return it to the pot. Add the cream, salt, and cayenne and stir. Reheat for a few minutes and serve hot with grated cheese as garnish.

During the warm weather, this soup can be refrigerated for a few hours and then served cold. When the soup is served hot, you can sprinkle some grated cheese on top of each serving.

Broccoli is unfortunately not a preferred vegetable among many people, in spite of its rich nutritional value. Not only is broccoli full of vitamins and minerals, but recent studies suggest eating it may prevent certain cancers, such as breast and colon cancer. Many people find broccoli more acceptable to the palate when served in the form of a creamy soup such as this one. Try it to teach your loved ones to love broccoli.

Irish Brotchan Soup

Ingredients   *6 servings*

4 tablespoons butter or margarine

4 leeks, chopped

4 parsnips, chopped

4 big potatoes, diced

3 pts, (1.7 l) water or stock
  (chicken or vegetable; add more
  if necessary)

2 bouillon cubes (not necessary if stock is used)

1¾ oz, (45g) chopped parsley

3 tablespoons lemon juice

3 tablespoons white wine

salt and pepper to taste

6 teaspoons sour cream as garnish

scallions, finely chopped, as garnish

1. Melt the butter in a soup pot and sauté the leeks slowly for a few minutes. Stir frequently. Add the parsnips and potatoes. Stir some more, cover the pot, and continue the sautéing for another 2 minutes.

2. Add the water or stock, the bouillon cubes, parsley, lemon juice, wine, salt, and pepper. Bring the soup to boil, place the lid over the pot, and simmer slowly for 40 minutes.

3. Let the soup cool, and then pass it through a sieve or blend in a blender. Return the soup to the pot. Check the seasonings, adding more lemon juice, salt, or pepper if necessary. Reheat the soup until it becomes very hot. Turn off the heat, cover the pot, and let the soup rest for 5 minutes before serving. Put 1 teaspoon of sour cream at the centre of each serving and surround it with finely chopped scallions as garnish. Serve immediately.

Minestrone Monastico

Ingredients   *6–8 servings*

5 pts, (2.8 l) water
3 carrots
3 potatoes
5 oz, (150g) green beans
2 celery stalks
5 oz, (150g) dry white beans
3 onions

8.5 fl oz, (240ml) olive oil
8.5 fl oz, (240ml) dry white wine
5 oz, (150g) macaroni
tarragon, minced
salt and pepper to taste
grated Parmesan cheese

1. Wash and peel the vegetables and cut them into small pieces (except the dry beans). Pour the water into a large soup pot and add all the vegetables (including beans) except the onions. Cook slowly over medium heat for 1 hour.
2. Sauté the onions in a bit of the olive oil in a large frying pan. When the onions begin to become golden, turn off the heat.
3. To the soup, add the onions, wine, the rest of the olive oil, macaroni, tarragon, salt, and pepper and continue cooking for another 15 minutes. Cover the pot and allow the soup to simmer for 10 minutes. Serve hot, with a side dish of grated Parmesan cheese.

In Italy, there are probably a thousand ways to prepare minestrone soup. Every household has a formula of its own. Minestrone has become quite popular in America and is often served at the monastic table as well. This particular version is proper to our monastery – hence the title of the recipe. Among the ingredients listed is a single cup of white wine, but one can easily add a cup or two more. The wine is the secret ingredient of this recipe – it makes all the difference in the world.

Potage Printanier à la Française

(French Spring Vegetable Soup)

3 tablespoons butter or margarine
4 oz, (100g)
  chopped cauliflower
3 oz, (75g) fresh peas
3.5 oz, (90g) chopped spinach
2 sliced carrots
2 leeks
3 pts 8 fl oz, (2 l) water,
  or more, if necessary

8.5 fl oz, (240ml) sherry wine
  or white wine of choice
2 bouillon cubes
2 sliced tomatoes, peeled and chopped
pinch mixed herbs (parsley, chervil and thyme)
1 chopped celeriac
salt and pepper to taste

1. Melt the butter in a soup pot and sauté the above vegetables for 1 or 2 minutes,
    except the tomatoes.
2. Add the water, sherry, bouillon cubes, peeled and chopped tomatoes, mixed herbs, salt,
    and pepper. Cook the soup slowly, covered, over low-medium heat for about 1 hour.
    Stir from time to time and add more water if necessary. Let the soup sit for 10 minutes.
3. When ready to serve, add some more fresh finely chopped herbs. Serve hot.

"Soup and fish explain half of the emotions of life."
– Sydney Smith

Saint Germain Pea soup

Ingredients   *6–8 servings*

16 oz, (450g) yellow or green split peas

3 pts 8 fl oz, (2 l) water

2 potatoes, peeled and diced

2 medium-sized turnips, diced

2 medium carrots, diced

2 celery stalks, thinly sliced

1 large onion, sliced

1 bay leaf

2 bouillon cubes

6 tablespoons olive oil or butter

salt and pepper to taste

croutons (see recipe p.195)

1. Soak the peas as directed on package and then drain. Put the water for the soup into a large soup pot and bring it to boil. Add the peas to the water. Also add the vegetables, bay leaf, and bouillon cubes. Cook over medium heat, covered, for about 1 hour, stirring from time to time. Let the soup cool.

2. Remove the bay leaf and blend the soup in a blender until it turns into a smooth cream. Pour the soup back into the pot. Add the oil, salt, pepper, and extra water or milk according to your preference. Bring the soup to boil again, stirring continuously, for 5 minutes. Let the soup sit, covered, for 5 minutes. Place the croutons in the individual soup plates and pour the soup on top of them. Serve hot.

80

Avacodo Velouté

Ingredients   *4–6 servings*

6 tablespoons butter
6 onions, sliced and minced
3 garlic cloves, minced
3 pts 8 fl oz, (2 l) water or broth
fresh corriander, chopped finely

2 avocados, peeled
6 tablespoons double cream (or cream and milk)
salt and pepper to taste
2 tablespoons brandy
4 eggs, separated

1. Melt the butter in a soup pot. Add the onions and garlic. Sauté slightly while stirring continually. Add the water and the brandy, cover the pot, and cook over low-medium heat for 30 minutes.
2. Blend the soup in a blender and return the contents to the pot. Beat the egg whites stiffly and add them to the soup while continuously stirring.
3. Place the egg yolks and the avocados in the blender and mix them thoroughly. Add this mixture, plus the salt and pepper, to the soup and continue stirring for a few minutes, until all the elements in the soup are well mixed. Continue cooking for 10 more minutes.
4. Add the cream and stir some more. Serve the velouté hot and sprinkle finely chopped corriander on top as garnish.

Saint Christopher Soup

Ingredients   *6 servings*

3 pts 8 fl oz, (2 l) vegetable broth
 (see recipe p.192)
½ medium-sized red cabbage,
 finely shredded and minced

8 tablespoons lemon juice
salt and pepper to taste

1.   Prepare a good vegetable broth.
2.   Place the finely chopped cabbage, lemon juice, salt, and pepper in a deep bowl.
     Let the mixture sit for an hour, stirring from time to time.
3.   Bring the broth to boil, add the cabbage and all the contents of the bowl, and cook for
     about 5 minutes. Serve immediately after.

This is a wonderful curative soup that is often used in France to ease indigestion problems or hangovers. It is a common remedy for many illnesses.

June

"What is one to say about June . . .
the time of perfect young summer,
the fulfilment of the promise of the earlier months,
and with as yet no sign to remind one that its fresh
young beauty will never fade?
For my own part I wander up into the wood and say:
'June is here – June is here: thank God for lovely June!'"

– Gertrude Jekyll

Soup from the Ardennes

Ingredients   *4–6 servings*

3 medium potatoes
2 leeks (white parts only)
2 shallots
3 endives
3 oz (75g) butter or margarine

2.5 pts, (1.4 l) milk
  (more if needed; can use skimmed)
salt and white pepper
nutmeg to taste
croutons (see recipe p. 195)

1. Peel the potatoes and cut them into thin slices. Slice the leeks, shallots, and endives very fine, julienne fashion.
2. Melt the butter in a saucepan, add the leeks, shallots, and endives, and sauté them for a few minutes. Add the milk and bring to a light boil. Add the potatoes, salt, pepper, and nutmeg. Lower the heat to low-medium and cook the soup for about 25 minutes, stirring from time to time.
3. Turn off the heat, cover the saucepan with a lid, and allow the soup to sit for 10 minutes.
4. Prepare croutons according to recipe on p. 195 or grill a few pieces of bread cubes to use as croutons. Place a few in each plate and pour the soup on top. Serve hot.

This is another soup that comes to us from the Belgian–northern French border. It is a soup that utilizes the classic vegetables of that region: leeks, endives, and potatoes. The very fact that the soup is prepared with milk rather than water enhances the quality and flavour of the soup. Those who may be concerned about the extra calories of the milk can easily substitute skim milk.

Cream of Fresh Greens Soup

Ingredients *6 servings*

6 tablespoons olive oil
1 onion, chopped
1 head lettuce or escarole, finely chopped
1 bunch watercress, finely chopped
16 oz, (450g) spinach, chopped
10 pts, (5.7 l) water,
  more if necessary

2 bouillon cubes
2 potatoes, sliced
17 fl oz, (480 ml) double cream
salt, nutmeg, and white pepper to taste
paprika as garnish

1. Pour the olive oil into the soup pot and sauté the onion slightly. Add the chopped greens, potatoes, bouillon cubes, and water. Boil the soup for 15 minutes and then simmer for another 15 minutes.

2. Blend the soup in a blender and return it to the pot. Add the heavy cream and seasonings and stir well. Reheat the soup and serve hot, sprinkling some paprika on top of each serving.

"Beautiful soup, so rich and green.
Waiting in a hot tureen!
Who for such dainties would not stoop?
Soup of the evening, beautiful soup!"

– Lewis Carroll, *Alice in Wonderland*

Oyster and Mushroom Soup

Ingredients

5 oz, (150g) shucked oysters
3 fl oz, (80ml) olive oil
2 shallots, chopped
6 oz, (180g) mushrooms,
  thinly sliced
8.5 fl oz, (240ml) dry vermouth
  or white wine

4 fl oz, (120ml) double cream
salt and pepper to taste
1 tablespoon tarragon
pinch dry mustard
grated lemon rind as garnish
1 pt 5 fl oz, (720ml) milk

1. Drain the oysters and place them aside.
2. Pour the oil into a pot and sauté the shallots and the mushrooms lightly for 2 to 3 minutes. Add the vermouth, stir well, cover pot, and continue cooking for 2 more minutes.
3. Add the oysters, milk, cream, salt, and pepper. Lower the heat to low-medium, cover the pot, and simmer the soup slowly for 20 minutes. Stir frequently and be sure the soup is boiling only very lightly.
4. Add the tarragon and a pinch of dry mustard. Stir well, cover the soup, and let it rest for 5 minutes before serving. Serve hot. Grate a lemon rind on top of the soup as garnish.

Danish Onion–Champagne Soup

10 onions, sliced
5 tablespoons butter or margarine or
   oil of choice
4 yolks of eggs
8.5 fl oz, (240ml) port wine
8 slices bread fried in butter

1 pt 14 fl oz, (1 l) dry champagne
half a Camembert cheese (or small Brie)
1 pt 14 fl oz, (960ml) boiling water
2 bay leaves
salt and fresh ground pepper to taste
dash cayenne pepper and nutmeg

1. Sauté the onions in butter until they begin to turn golden. Add the cups of boiling water, salt, pepper, and a dash of cayenne and nutmeg. Add also the bay leaves. Stir well and bring the water to another boil. Reduce the heat to low-medium and cook, covered, for 20 minutes.
2. Add the entire bottle of champagne and bring the soup to yet another boil. Then add the cheese and take care to mix it well in the boiling soup.
3. Beat the egg yolks together with the port wine and add the egg-wine mixture to the soup. Stir well. Turn off the heat and let the soup rest, covered, for 10 minutes. (The soup must not boil again after the egg-wine mixture has been added.)
4. Place 1 slice of fried bread in the centre of each bowl and ladle the soup on top of it. Serve hot.

Northern Europe is well known for soups made with beer. This soup from Denmark, however, makes use of champagne, which gives the soup a particular flavour all its own. Since champagne is expensive, I recommend a local, more ordinary type of sparkling wine, not the costly authentic champagne imported from France. This is an excellent soup to serve when one has a congenial and informal group of friends over for a meal. But since it is quite heavy, the rest of the menu should be light though equally appetizing.

Potato Dumpling Soup

1 onion
1 carrot
1 celery stalk
4 mushrooms
6 tablespoons oil
2 pts, (1.2 l) water
salt and pepper to taste

Dumplings:
12 oz, (360g) mashed potatoes
1 teaspoon salt
1 egg
1 tablespoon chopped parsley
2.5 oz, (75g) flour

1. Slice the vegetables thinly and sauté them slowly in the oil for a few minutes in a soup pot. Add the water gradually, stirring continuously. Add salt and pepper. Cover the pot and cook over low-medium heat for 30 minutes.
2. While the soup is cooking, combine all the ingredients for the dumplings. Roll the paste into a thin long cylinder. Cut into 1-inch lengths and roll them in the palms of your hands.
3. Drop the dumplings into the soup and continue cooking for another 8 to 10 minutes. Serve hot.

Greek Spartan Soup

Ingredients   *4–6 servings*

1 pt 14 fl oz, (960ml) beef broth
3 pts 8 fl oz, (2 l) water
2 leeks, sliced julienne style
2 carrots, sliced julienne style
1 celery stalk, thinly sliced
1 small cabbage, shredded

1 large onion, sliced
1 garlic clove, minced
2 lemons
4 eggs
salt and pepper to taste

1. Pour the broth and the water into a large soup pot. Add all the vegetables and bring to a gentle boil. Lower the heat to low-medium and simmer the soup for 1½ hours, covered. Add more water, if needed. Skim all the white part that rises in the soup carefully and discard it.
2. Squeeze the juice from the 2 lemons and add it to the soup. Beat the eggs carefully and mix them with the soup. Add the seasonings and stir quickly for 2 or 3 minutes. Serve the soup immediately.

Despite its name, there is nothing "Spartan" about this soup. Everyone who has tried this recipe assures me it is very rich and very filling. This soup is a complete meal in itself, or a *repas complet*, as it is called in France. The eggs add a full meal's worth of protein. A light salad of mixed greens and a piece of fresh fruit following the soup should be enough to satisfy anyone, no matter how hungry.

Chervil Soup

2 leeks
1¾ oz, (45g) chopped celery
2 tablespoons butter, margarine,
  or oil of choice
4 potatoes, diced

1 pt 14 fl oz, (1 l) water
17 fl oz, (480ml) milk
5 oz, (150g) fresh chopped chervil
salt and pepper to taste

1. Wash and cut the leeks and celery into thin pieces. Melt the butter in a soup pot.
   Add the leeks, celery, and potatoes. Sauté for 2 to 3 minutes. Add the water and cook,
   covered, over low-medium heat until the soup is done.
2. Add the remaining ingredients and purée the soup in a blender. Bring the soup to boil
   again, stirring continuously. Serve immediately. Soup can also be refrigerated and
   served cold during the hot weather.

Solyanka

(Cucumber–Fish Soup)

Ingredients   *4–6 servings*

2 large cucumbers (fresh or pickled)
3 tablespoons butter or margarine
2 onions, chopped
2.5 pts, (1.4 l) water
4 fl oz, (120ml) vodka
2 white fish fillets (cod or haddock)
  cut into small chunks

2 teaspoons chopped capers
1 bay leaf
1 oz, (25g) green olives, pitted and chopped
salt and pepper to taste
garnish: 1 lemon cut in thin slices,
  fresh parsley (or dill), finely chopped

1. Peel and halve the cucumber. Scoop out the seeds. Cut the cucumber into thin slices, sprinkle them with salt, and place them in a bowl in the refrigerator for at least 8 hours. Rinse and drain the slices before adding them to the soup.
2. Melt the butter in a soup pot and sauté the onions over moderate heat for 2 to 3 minutes. Add the water, vodka, fish chunks, and bay leaf. Bring the water to boil, cover the pot, and cook the soup for 20 minutes.
3. Add the cucumber slices, capers, olives, salt, and pepper. Cover the pot and simmer for another 20 minutes.
4. Turn off the heat, remove the bay leaf, and serve the soup immediately. Garnish each plate with 2 lemon slices and some finely chopped parsley.

"The classification of traditional Russian soups has been traced to 16th and 17th century annals. Solyanka was originally applied to any food by the peasantry. Today Solyanka denotes a savoury, tart soup in which sauerkraut or pickled cucumbers are one of the main ingredients."

– F Siegel, *Russian Cooking*

Cream of Cauliflower Soup

16 oz, (450g) fresh cauliflower
2 potatoes
1 large carrot
1 onion
2 garlic cloves, chopped

1 bouillon cube
3 pts 8 fl oz, (2 l) water
17 fl oz, (480ml) white sauce (see recipe p.194)
salt and pepper to taste
chopped chervil as garnish

1. Wash vegetables and slice into small pieces. Put the water in a large pot and add all the vegetables, the chopped garlic, and the bouillon cube. Cook slowly, covered, over low-medium heat for 1 hour. Add more water if necessary.
2. In a medium-sized pot, prepare 2 cups (17 fl oz, 480ml) of white sauce according to the recipe on p.194.
3. After the vegetables are cooked, blend the soup in a blender and then pour back into the pot. Add the white sauce and seasonings according to taste.
   Stir the soup thoroughly.
4. Reheat the soup for a few minutes to serve hot (during the winter months).
   During the warm months, refrigerate the soup for 4 or more hours and serve cold.
   Sprinkle chopped chervil on top as garnish.

Cauliflower has a wonderful mild taste that doesn't overpower the palate. This particular soup can be prepared and enjoyed all year round, since fresh cauliflower is readily available everywhere. If you decide to serve it during the summer months, then be sure to chill it first for several hours before serving.

Zuppa di Pasta e Fagioli
(Pasta and Bean Soup)

Ingredients   *4–6 servings*

2 medium-sized onions, finely chopped

3 fl oz, (80ml) olive oil

4 garlic cloves, minced

1 28-oz, (775g) can Italian tomatoes, chopped, with juice

1 bay leaf

1 teaspoon dried rosemary

1 teaspoon fresh or dried basil, chopped

4 sprigs fresh Italian parsley, chopped

1lb, (450g) precooked white beans (cannellini) or the equivalent in canned beans 1 15-oz, (450g) can

2.5 pts, (1.4 l) water

8.5 fl oz, (250ml) white wine

salt and freshly ground pepper to taste

4 oz dried pasta (small shells are best)

grated Parmesan or Romano cheese as garnish

1. Sauté the onions in olive oil in a large-sized soup pot for about 2 minutes. Add the garlic and sauté for another minute, stirring continually.

2. Add the chopped tomatoes (with their juice), bay leaf, rosemary, basil, and parsley. Cook over medium heat for about 3 minutes, until the mixture attains a smooth, thick consistency. Stir often.

3. Add the precooked beans, water, wine, salt, and pepper. Stir the soup well and bring it to boil. Cook for about 15 minutes, covered, over medium heat. (Do not overcook.) Add the pasta and continue cooking for another 5 minutes. Turn off the heat, cover the pot, and let the soup rest for about 10 minutes. Serve hot. Remove the bay leaf. Sprinkle some grated cheese on the top of each serving. For that extra Italian touch, add 1 tablespoon olive oil in the centre of the bowl.

Additions may be made to this soup, e.g., other vegetables or pancetta (bacon), according to taste.

Carrot Soup à la Normande

Ingredients   *6 servings*

2 onions
8 carrots   ve oil
2.5 pints, (1.4 l) water   taste
8.5 fl oz, (250ml) mil   on juice
3 tablespoons flour   finely minced parsley

Too Bland use stock not water

1. Chop onions and carrots finely, put in soup pot, and add water. Cook slowly, bringing the water to boil. Then let the soup sit, covered, for 20 minutes.
2. Add the milk, flour, thyme, oil, salt, and pepper. Blend in a blender and pour the soup back into the pot. Add the lemon juice. Cook slowly for about 10 minutes, until hot. Serve the soup with parsley sprinkled on top. It can be served hot or cold. (Refrigerate for a few hours if you decide to serve it cold.)

Exotic Chinese Cucumber Soup

Ingredients   *4–6 servings*

2.5 pts, (1.4 l) chicken or vegetable broth
2 good-sized cucumbers, peeled, seeded, and diced
8 mushrooms, washed and thinly sliced
4 scallions, chopped

salt and pepper to taste
8 teaspoons sesame oil
1 tablespoon white vinegar
  or rice vinegar
pinch ginger powder

1. Place the broth in a soup pot and bring it to the boiling point. Add the cucumbers, mushrooms, scallions, salt, and pepper. Cover the soup pot and cook gently over low-medium heat for 15 to 20 minutes.
2. Blend the soup in a blender. Add the extra seasonings – sesame oil, vinegar, and ginger – and blend well. Refrigerate the soup for a few hours and serve cold. Or reheat the soup and serve it hot, as the Chinese do.

"For people not familiar with Chinese or Japanese broths, these can be described either as extremely delicate or as appearing to be made with no ingredients at all. Beef or chicken broth made according to Oriental recipes is like English beef tea made with lean soup meat and herbs and simmered for hours below the boiling point – this to keep the broth clear without having to strain it or clarify it with eggshells."
– Dolores Vanetti, *The Querulous Cook*

95

Spanish Corriander Soup

Ingredients *6 servings*

6 tablespoons olive oil
2 onions, chopped
2 leeks (whites only), chopped
4 potatoes, peeled and cubed
3 pts, (1.7 l)
   vegetable or chicken broth

3.5 oz, (90g) coarsely chopped fresh
   corriander – save some for garnish
3 garlic cloves, minced
pinch of cayenne pepper to taste
salt to taste

1. Pour the olive oil into a soup pot and sauté the onions, leeks, and garlic lightly over low heat for 2 to 3 minutes. Add the cubed potatoes and continue sautéing for 1 extra minute while stirring constantly.
2. Add the broth, cover the pot, and simmer the soup for 30 minutes, or until the potatoes are thoroughly cooked. Remove from the heat.
3. Add the fresh corriander and also the salt and cayenne pepper. Blend the soup in a blender or food processor about one third of the amount at a time. Refrigerate the soup for at least 10 hours before serving. Serve the soup very cold with some fresh corriander leaves on top of each serving as garnish.

Celery–Orange Velouté

Ingredients *4–6 servings*

8 celery stalks, chopped
2.5 pts, (1.4 l) water
1 pt 14 fl oz, (960ml)
  orange juice
1 bouillon cube (vegetable)
salt and pepper to taste

2 egg yolks
4 fl oz, (120ml) white vermouth (dry)
1 teaspoon flour
2 tablespoons crème fraîche or sour cream
½ teaspoon sugar
fresh mint leaves as garnish

1. Wash, clean, and chop the celery stalks. Place them in a soup pot. Add the water, orange juice, bouillon cube, salt, and pepper. Bring to boil, then cover the pot and cook at a gentle boil for 1½ to 2 hours. Pass the soup through a colander and remove the solids.
2. Beat the egg yolks in a deep bowl. Add the vermouth, flour, crème fraîche, and sugar and mix thoroughly (better yet, blend it in a blender until thick and creamy).
3. Pour the mixture into the soup and stir thoroughly until it is all well blended. Check the seasonings and reheat the soup until it is hot. (Do not let it come to boil!) Serve immediately, placing a few fresh mint leaves on each serving as garnish. (This soup is always refreshing, even when it is served hot during the summer months.)

Chilled Carrot Soup

Ingredients   *4 servings*

2 leeks, chopped
2 potatoes, peeled and diced
4 good-sized carrots, sliced
1 pt 9 fl oz, (850ml)
  chicken or vegetable stock
salt to taste

½ teaspoon ginger powder
4 tablespoons lemon juice
8.5 fl oz, (240ml) single cream
thin slices of lemon or fresh mint
leaves as garnish

1. Place the prepared vegetables in a soup pot, add stock and salt, and bring the soup to boil. Reduce the heat and simmer, covered, until the vegetables are well cooked.
2. Add the ginger, lemon juice, and cream. Stir well.
3. Blend the soup in a blender or food processor and then chill the soup for a few hours before serving. Serve the soup in glass bowls and garnish each with a thin lemon slice or with fresh mint leaves.

98

July

"O summer day beside the joyous sea!
O summer day so wonderful and white,
So full of gladness and so full of pain!
Forever and forever shall thou be
To some the gravestone of a dead delight,
To some the landmark of a new domain."

– Henry Wadsworth Longfellow

Saint Bertille Herb Soup

Ingredients

1 small head leaf lettuce
1 bunch sorrel
3.5 oz, (90g) chopped parsley
10 scallions or 2 leeks
1 bunch watercress
butter
1 oz, (25g) chervil

2.5 pts, (1.4 l) water
  (or vegetable stock if served hot)
8.5 fl oz, (240ml) white wine
4 fl oz, (120ml) double cream
  (or half cream & milk for lighter option)
1 egg yolk, beaten
salt and pepper to taste

1. Shred the lettuce and the sorrel. Chop the parsley, scallions, and watercress into small pieces.
2. Melt the butter in the soup pot, add the chopped greens, and cook slowly for a few minutes over low heat. Stir continually. Add the water (or stock) and the wine. Cover the pot and cook for about 40 minutes.
3. Remove the pot from the heat, add the cream, beaten egg, chervil, salt, and pepper. Blend well in a blender. Reheat the soup for a few minutes, but do not allow it to boil. Refrigerate the soup and serve cold. Or it can be served hot with slices of French bread on the side.

"Many soups that evolved through the centuries, in the French provinces, are based more on vegetables than on meats and are described as 'healthy' potages de sante . . . These soups depend on spinach and sorrel, and all the herbs, and mushrooms, and fresh milk and cream and butter, all tasting perennially and incredibly delicious after the long dark months of eating stored roots, like turnips, and potatoes and cabbages and onions and garlic."
– M. E. K. Fisher, *The Cooking of Provincial*

Cream of Vegetable Soup à la Mode de Tours

Ingredients *6 servings*

4 large carrots
4 medium-sized white turnips
3 leeks (white parts only)
4 tablespoons butter, or margarine, or oil of choice
3 pts, (1.7 l) water

4 oz, (112g) rice
3 oz, (75g) peas, fresh or frozen
17 fl oz, (480ml) milk
salt and pepper to taste
crème fraîche and chopped chervil as garnish
2 large potatoes, peeled and sliced

1. Wash and slice finely the carrots, turnips, and leeks.
2. Melt the butter in a soup pot and sauté the vegetables briefly for 2 or 3 minutes. Stir continually. Add the water and bring it to boil. Lower the heat to medium and cook, covered, for about 15 minutes.
3. Add the potatoes, rice, and peas and stir. Cover the pot and continue cooking for another 30 minutes, this time over low-medium heat.
4. Strain the soup and pass the vegetables through a sieve or blend in a blender. Return the liquid part and the vegetables to the soup pot. Add the milk and the seasonings and bring the soup to a light boil while stirring often. Turn off the heat and let the soup stand, covered, for 5 minutes. Serve the soup hot during the winter months or refrigerate for a few hours and serve it cold during the summer. If the soup is served cold, it is better to use a light oil instead of butter. Garnish the soup with a teaspoon of crème fraîche (or sour cream) at the centre and some finely chopped chervil all around.

Consommé of Celeriac

Ingredients   *4–6 servings*

2–3 celeriacs
3 pts 8 fl oz, (2 l) water
3 bouillon cubes, or chicken stock
3 tomatoes
2 lemons

1 celery heart
parsley
pinch of cayenne
salt to taste

1. Cut the celeriacs into big chunks and cook them slowly in the water over medium heat. Add the bouillon cubes and continue to cook.
2. Peel the tomatoes and strain them through a colander, discarding the seeds. Add this mixture and the juice from the lemons to the soup.
3. Slice the celery heart into thin small pieces. Chop the parsley, then mince the celery and parsley together and add them to the soup. Add the cayenne and salt.
4. After 1 hour and 15 minutes of cooking, taste and see if the soup is done. Then strain it through a thin colander, separating the solid vegetables. Place the consommé in the refrigerator for several hours. Serve cold.

"With a knowledge of blended flavours, the French have combined imagination and a flair for seasoning, so that their soups are worthy of imitation."
– Claire de Pratz, *French Home Cooking*

Jerusalem Artichoke Soup

Ingredients   *6 servings*

3 pts 8 fl oz, (2 l) water
10 Jerusalem artichokes,
  well-washed and sliced
5 large potatoes, peeled and sliced
1 leek, thinly sliced
2 onions, chopped

2 garlic cloves, minced
6 tablespoons oil of choice or butter or margarine
17 fl oz, (480ml) milk
salt and pepper to taste
fresh chopped parsley as garnish

1. Pour water into a soup pot and add the Jerusalem artichokes and potatoes.
    Cover the pot, bring the water to boil, and then reduce the heat to low-medium.
    Simmer gently for 45 minutes.

2. Slice the leek and onions and mince the garlic. Place them in a separate pot, add the oil
    or butter, and sauté over low heat with the pan covered for about 2 or 3 minutes,
    maximum. Stir frequently, and see that the vegetables don't burn or stick to the pan.

3. Add the leek-garlic-onion mixture to the soup and continue cooking for an added 15
    minutes. Turn off the heat and allow the soup to cool.

4. Blend the soup in a blender or food processor or pass it through a sieve. Return the
    soup to a clean pot and add the seasonings and the milk. Mix well and reheat the soup,
    bringing it to boil. Turn off the heat, cover the pot, and let the soup rest for 5 minutes
    before serving. Garnish each serving with fresh chopped parsley on the top. (This soup
    can be refrigerated for a few hours and served cold during the summer months.)

Colbert Clear Soup

Ingredients

4 servings

3 pts 8 fl oz, (2 l) water
4 bouillon cubes
2 carrots
2 leeks or onions

2 tablespoons lemon juice
4 fl oz, (120ml) white vermouth
salt and pepper to taste
1 bunch sorrel leaves (or spinach leaves)

1. Bring the water to boil. Add the bouillon cubes, sliced carrots, leeks, sorrel, lemon juice, vermouth, and salt and pepper. Cook soup slowly for 1 hour and 15 minutes. Let it stand for 15 minutes, then strain it through a colander.
2. Refrigerate the consommé for several hours and serve it very cold.

"All of us know that the water in which vegetables have been cooked contains valuable mineral matter. It hurts us to throw it out, but we do not want to serve it with the vegetables. The soup pot waits for such things, and in proportion as it receives them is the soup rich and tasty. Its success does not depend upon accurate measurements and specific ingredients but upon blended flavours."

– Claire de Pratz, *French Home Cooking*

Cold Tomato Soup

Ingredients   *4–6 servings*

3 fl oz, (90ml) olive oil
4 leeks (white part only)
8 large tomatoes
4 minced garlic cloves
bouquet garni (a few sprigs of tarragon,
    thyme, and basil tied together and
    removed before serving the soup)

Salt and pepper to taste
dash of lemon juice
1 celery stalk, chopped and minced
    (optional)
3 pts 8 fl oz, (2 l) water

1. Pour the oil into a large soup pot. Add the sliced leeks, garlic, and tomatoes, peeled and sliced into quarters. Sauté for a few minutes until the tomatoes dissolve into a sauce.
2. Add water and the remaining ingredients. Cover the pot and let the soup cook over medium heat for about 30 minutes. Strain the soup through a sieve and refrigerate it for at least 3 hours. Serve very chilled.

Shrimp and Corn Chowder

Ingredients   *6 servings*

2 pts, (1.2 l) water
2 onions, chopped
2 celery stalks, chopped
1 small chopped green pepper
1 finely diced carrot
2 large potatoes, diced
1 bay leaf

17 fl oz, (480ml) milk
1 17-oz, (500g) can creamed corn
3 oz, (75g) whole-kernel corn
16 oz, (450g) shelled shrimps, cooked
salt and pepper to taste
finely chopped parsley and paprika (as garnish)
2 tablespoons flour

1. Pour the water into a large soup pot. Add the onions, celery, pepper, carrot, potatoes, and bay leaf. Bring to boil and then simmer slowly, covered, for about 20 minutes.
2. Dilute the flour in milk and add to the soup.
3. Add the corn, cooked shrimp, and seasonings. Blend and stir the soup, cooking for a few minutes over low-medium heat. Remove the bay leaf. Serve the soup, garnishing each bowl with a sprinkle of chopped parsley and paprika.

"In 15 intervening years I had forgotten how delicious was this shrimp and corn chowder. I have since made it with both fresh and frozen corn – and can hardly tell which is which. I have also used frozen shrimps with excellent results . . . The thin white sauce that gives the chowder its special creaminess is made separately and brought together with the other ingredients in the preparation."

– Bernard Clayton, Jr., *The Complete Book of Soups and Stews*

Consommé Madrilène

Ingredients   *4–6 servings*

3 pts 8 fl oz, (2 l) water
4 bouillon cubes
4 celery stalks, sliced and minced
2 medium onions, minced
2 tomatoes, peeled and sliced

1 green pepper, sliced
1 10oz, (275g) can tomato sauce
dash of cayenne
salt and pepper to taste

1. Bring the water to boil and add bouillon cubes, prepared vegetables, the can of tomato sauce, cayenne, salt, and pepper. Boil slowly over low-medium heat for 1 hour 15 minutes. Let stand for another 10 minutes.
2. Strain the consommé through a colander. Refrigerate for several hours. Serve cold.

Avocado Soup

Ingredients   *4 servings*

2 avocados (ripe)
8.5 fl oz, (240ml) skimmed milk
  (or single cream for a thicker soup)
4 tablespoons scallions, minced
1 teaspoon lemon juice

1 pt 5 fl oz, (720ml) chicken broth
2 fl oz, (60ml) dry sherry
salt and white pepper to taste
1 oz, (25g) corriander, minced

1. Cut the avocados in half. Pit, peel, and cut them into chunks. Blend the avocado chunks and the milk in a blender. Add the scallions and lemon juice and blend again until the mixture becomes smooth.
2. Bring the chicken broth to boil. Turn off the heat and add the sherry, salt, pepper, and half of the corriander. Let it simmer for a few minutes.
3. Pour the avocado mixture into the broth and mix thoroughly. Allow the soup to be refrigerated for at least 2 hours. Serve the soup cold, and garnish with the remaining corriander before serving.

This is a wonderful and nutritious soup for the summertime, and serves as a delectable appetizer to a good summer meal. Vegetarians may wish to substitute vegetable broth for the chicken broth. Nutrition-wise, keep in mind that avocado contains complete protein.

Cold Salmon Chowder

Ingredients   *4 servings*

1 pt 14 fl oz, (1 l) low-fat milk
  (more if necessary)
1 onion, sliced
1 celery stalk, sliced
1 small red pepper, diced
1 cup (7oz, 200g) fresh salmon,
  lightly poached

4 fl oz, (120ml) single cream
4 teaspoons dry sherry
salt and white pepper to taste
cucumber slices as garnish
some chopped dill

1. Pour the milk into a soup pot and cook thinly sliced vegetables for about 10 minutes, stirring continually.
2. Remove all the bones and skin from the salmon, flake it, and add it to the soup. Add the cream, sherry, and seasonings. With an electric mixer, blend the soup thoroughly. Place it in the refrigerator and chill it for at least 8 to 10 hours.
3. As you ladle the chowder into the soup plates, garnish each one with a cucumber slice and some finely chopped dill.

This is an easy recipe to prepare and serve during the hot days of summer. The word "chowder" has its roots in the French word chaudière, a 3-legged heavy iron pot used to prepare thick soups. It is very probable that the word migrated from French Canada to New England and later to Long Island, New York, where all varieties of thick seafood soups go by the name of chowder.

Pea and Carrot Minted Soup

Ingredients   *4–6 servings*

1 lb 4 oz, (550g) peas, fresh or frozen
2 carrots, peeled and sliced
2 leeks, or 1 onion, chopped
2 pts, (1.2 l) vegetable or
  chicken stock
1 tablespoon sugar
8 fresh mint leaves

3 tablespoons butter or margarine or oil of choice
2 tablespoons cornstarch
8.5 fl oz, (240ml) milk (low-fat can be used)
salt and pepper to taste
fresh mint leaves as garnish

1. Place prepared vegetables in the soup pot and add the stock. Bring the soup to a boil, add the sugar, mint leaves, salt, and pepper, and then cover the pot. Simmer the soup over low heat for 30 minutes.
2. Blend the soup in a blender or food processor until it is thoroughly puréed.
3. Melt the butter in a separate pot, add the cornstarch, and stir continually until it turns into a paste. Add the milk and continue stirring until it thickens.
4. Add the sauce to the pea soup and blend thoroughly. Reheat the soup and serve it hot with a few mint leaves on the top of each serving as garnish. (This soup can also be refrigerated for a few hours and served cold.)

Neapolitan Courgette Soup

Ingredients   *6 servings*

7 small courgettes, sliced
3 tablespoons butter
2.5 pts, (1.4 l) water
salt and pepper to taste

4 tablespoons grated Parmesan cheese
bunch of parsley and basil, finely chopped
croutons (optional; see recipe p.195)
3 eggs

1. Place the finely sliced courgettes in a good-sized soup pot. Add the butter and cook slowly over low heat for about 5 minutes. Stir constantly.
2. Add the water, salt, and pepper, bring to the boil, and continue cooking until the courgette are tender (about 20 minutes). Cover the pot.
3. Beat the eggs in a large bowl, add the cheese, chopped parsley, and basil, and mix it all thoroughly. Add the mixture to the soup and stir. Allow it to cook for another 4 to 5 minutes, maximum.
4. Serve hot, adding some croutons on top as garnish.

Cold Basil Soup

Ingredients   *6 servings*

2 medium-sized cucumbers, peeled,
 seeded and sliced
3 green bell peppers (sweet), sliced
4 medium-sized tomatoes, sliced
1 white sweet onion, sliced
2 garlic cloves, peeled

25 basil leaves, washed
2 pts, (1.2 l) cold water
1 16 oz, (450g) container of plain yogurt
salt and pepper to taste
fresh basil leaves as garnish

1. Place the prepared vegetables, garlic, and basil leaves in a blender and mix
   all of it thoroughly.
2. Pour the contents of the blender into a large soup pot or a large bowl.
   Add the water, salt, pepper, and yogurt and mix all of it well by hand. Refrigerate the
   soup for at least 3 hours before serving.
3. Serve the soup in deep bowls. Place some fresh basil leaves in the centre as garnish.

August

"The quiet August noon has come;
A slumbrous silence fills the sky,
The fields are still, the woods are dumb,
In glassy sleep the water lies.

"Beneath the open sky abroad,
Among the plants and breathing things,
The sinless, peaceful works of God,
I'll share the calm the season brings."

– William Cullen Bryant

113

Cream of Fennel Soup

1 leek, thinly sliced
3 fl oz, (90ml) olive oil
4 garlic cloves, minced
5 fennel bulbs, thinly sliced
8 tomatoes, peeled, seeded,
  and chopped
2.5 pts, (1.4 l) water
  (or vegetable or chicken stock)

3 bouillon cubes (if stock not available)
1¾ oz, (45g) top greens from the fennel,
  chopped finely in a food processor
8.5 fl oz, (240ml) double cream
  or low-fat yogurt
salt and pepper to taste

1. Sauté the leeks in the oil until tender. Add immediately the garlic and the fennel. Stir well and cook for a few minutes, until the fennel begins to soften.
2. Add the tomatoes. Stir well and cook over moderate heat until the tomatoes are dissolved and turn into a sauce. Add the water or stock. Bring to boil and cook over medium heat for 15 minutes.
3. Blend the soup in a blender and then return it to the soup pot. Add the processed fennel greens, cream, salt, and pepper. Bring to boil again for 1 minute. Turn off the heat, stir well, cover the pot, and let the soup rest for 10 minutes before serving. During the summer months, chill the soup in the refrigerator for 1 hour and serve cold.

This is an unusual and elegant soup, usually served cold during the summer months. The liquorice taste of the fennel is simultaneously subtle, refreshing, and striking. Weight–watchers may easily substitute low fat yogurt for the double cream. Or, better yet, use half a cup (4 fl oz, 120ml) of regular yogurt and half a cup (4 fl oz, 120ml) of low fat milk.

Garlic Consommé

3 pts 8 fl oz, (2 l) water (or meat stock)
3 bouillon cubes (if stock not used)
12 cloves garlic, minced
1 bouquet garni (bay leaf, thyme, parsley,
  oregano tied together and removed
  before serving the soup)

1 10 oz , (275g) can tomato sauce
2 fl oz, (60ml) brandy
pinch of cayenne
salt to taste

1. Bring the water to boil. Add bouillon cubes, garlic, and bouquet garni. Cover and allow
    to cook over low heat for 1 hour or more. Add more water if necessary.
2. After 1 hour of slow cooking, add the tomato sauce, brandy, cayenne, and salt.
    Stir, making sure to mix well. Strain and discard the garlic and bouquet garni.
    Serve hot during the cold months or refrigerate and serve cold during the warm months.

Broccoli Soup

Ingredients   *4 servings*

16 oz, (450g) broccoli   6 tablespoons olive oil
3 garlic cloves   1 6 oz, (175g) can tomato paste
2.5 pts, (1.4 l) water   salt and pepper to taste
6 parsley sprigs   Gruyère or Parmesan cheese, grated
4 strips lean bacon

1. Wash the broccoli thoroughly. Slice it in small pieces, discarding the tough part of the stalks. Chop well the garlic, parsley, and bacon.
2. Pour the olive oil into a soup pot, add the broccoli, garlic, parsley, and bacon, and sauté them for a minute or two while stirring at the same time. Add the tomato paste and 2 cups (17 fl oz, 480ml) water. Stir well. Cover the pot and allow the soup to cook for about 5 minutes.
3. Add the remaining water and cook the soup over medium heat for about 30 minutes. Add salt and pepper and simmer for a few minutes. Just before serving, purée the soup in a blender. The soup can be served hot or cold. If it is served hot, garnish the soup at the last minute with some grated cheese.

This is a very quick and easy soup to prepare, and an all-time favourite among our monastery guests. It can be served at any time of the year. When served cold, it should be refrigerated for at least 2 hours, and instead of the grated cheese, one may add 1 teaspoon of sour cream to each serving bowl as garnish.

Soup Pelou

(Radish Greens Soup)

Ingredients   *4 servings*

3 fl oz, (90ml) olive oil
2 leeks or onions, chopped
1 bunch fresh radish tops and leaves
  (or mustard or turnip greens)
4 potatoes, peeled and cubed

2 pts, (1.2 l) water
salt and pepper to taste
¼ teaspoon nutmeg
4 fl oz, (120ml) milk
croutons as garnish

1. Pour the olive oil into a pot and add the leeks. Sauté lightly over low-medium heat
   for 3 minutes. Add immediately the well-washed and chopped radish tops.
   Stir. Cover the pot, and let the sautéing process continue for another 3 minutes.
2. Add the potatoes, water, salt, pepper, and nutmeg and stir again very well.
   Cover the pot and simmer the soup for 45 minutes. Allow the soup to cool.
3. Pass the soup through a sieve or blend it in a blender, and then return it to a clean pot.
   Add the milk and mix well. Reheat the soup if you wish to serve it hot, or refrigerate it
   for a few hours and serve cold.

Parsley Soup

Ingredients   *4 serving*

4 medium tomatoes   8.5 fl oz, (240ml) white dry wine
5 tablespoons olive oil   2 pts, (1 l) water
1 leek, finely chopped   salt and pepper to taste
1 onion, chopped and minced   1 big bunch parsley (finely chopped, preferably
4 garlic cloves, minced   the leafy Italian type)

1. Wash the tomatoes. Boil them for a few minutes and then peel. Slice them lengthwise
    and discard the seeds.
2. Pour the olive oil into a soup pot. Add the leek and onion and sauté for a few minutes,
    until they begin to turn golden. Add the tomatoes, garlic, wine, water, salt, and pepper.
    Allow to boil over low-medium heat for 20 minutes. Add the parsley and continue
    cooking for another 10 minutes. Blend the soup in a blender. Serve hot or refrigerate for
    a few hours and serve cold.

"Parsley is most frequently used either chopped or in the leaf as a
garnish for dishes, but it is delicious when used in large quantities
as a pronounced seasoning. Like mint, it is one of the easiest of herbs to
grow. Generally, there are two kinds of parsley available, the curly
variety and the flat leaf, which is also called Italian parsley. Raw parsley
is said to sweeten the breath."

– C. Claiborne, *An Herb and Spice Cook Book*

Gazpacho

Ingredients   *6 servings*

4 large tomatoes, peeled, seeded,
  and coarsely cut up
2 cucumbers peeled, seeded, and
  coarsely cut up
1 large green pepper
2 red onions, coarsely cut up
1 cup (8.5 fl oz, 240ml) dry sherry
2 tablespoons red wine vinegar

1oz, (25g) finely chopped parsley
2 slices stale bread, crumbled
4 fl oz, (120ml) olive oil
2 tablespoons finely chopped celery leaves
salt and fresh ground pepper to taste
3 pts 8 fl oz, (2 l) water
4 minced garlic cloves

1. Prepare tomatoes and place on a separate plate. Prepare the cucumbers, sprinkle with
    salt, and place on a separate plate. Dice the green pepper and 1 of the red onions and
    place each on a separate plate.
2. Bring the water to boil in a large soup pot, adding half the diced tomatoes, the other red
    onion, minced garlic cloves, parsley, stale bread, olive oil, celery leaves, and salt and
    pepper. Let it boil over medium heat for about 30 minutes. Cool it and add the dry
    sherry and vinegar and blend the soup in a blender. Refrigerate for about 4 hours.
3. When it's time to serve the soup, pass around individual plates with the diced tomatoes,
    pepper, cucumber, and onion. They can be added individually according to taste.

Garden Borscht

Ingredients   *6–8 serving*

2 tablespoons oil
2 carrots, diced
1 onion, diced
1 10½ oz, (275g) can vegetable juice
2 pts 6 fl oz, (1.3 l) water
1½ pounds (670g) beets, peeled and
  coarsely shredded

2 celery stalks, thinly sliced
1 6 oz, (175g) can tomato paste
3 tablespoons sugar
2 tomatoes, peeled and chopped
2 fl oz, (60ml) cider vinegar
2 teaspoons salt
sour cream as garnish

1. Put the oil into a large soup pot. Cook the celery, carrots, and onion over medium heat until tender, stirring frequently. Add the vegetable juice, water, and the remaining ingredients except the sour cream. Bring the soup to boiling point, then reduce heat to low.
2. Cover and simmer for 50 minutes or until the vegetables are tender. Stir often. Refrigerate and serve cold.
3. Just before serving, put a dash of sour cream in the centre of the soup.

Borscht originated among the Russian peasants, and there are hundreds of varieties of this soup. This particular version is well adapted for summertime, and it should be chilled for several hours before serving. The classic borscht is a robust thick soup where vegetables, especially beets, are the main staple. In the summer, I use freshly picked beets from our garden for extra-special flavour.

Consommé Belle Fermière

(Farmer Vegetable Soup)

Ingredients   *4–6 servings*

5 pts, (2.8 l) water (more if needed)   4 bouillon cubes
1 small head cabbage   8 tablespoons olive oil
1 large onion   1 bay leaf
2 carrots   salt and pepper to taste
10 French-cut string beans

1.   Bring the water to boil in a soup pot. Add the vegetables sliced in small pieces.
     Add the bouillon cubes, oil, bay leaf, salt, and pepper to taste.
2.   After 1 hour and 15 minutes of slow cooking, turn off the heat and let the consommé
     sit, covered, for 15 to 20 minutes. Drain the vegetables, pour the consommé back into
     the pot, and bring to boil. Serve hot, or refrigerate for several hours and serve cold.

Potage Crécy

(Carrot Potage)

Ingredients   *6 servings*

10 carrots	1 tablespoon tomato paste
1 potato	1 tablespoon butter
1 onion	1 teaspoon sugar
3 pts 8 fl oz, (2 l) water	salt and pepper to taste
(or vegetable stock)	2 tablespoons double cream (optional)
1 cube vegetable bouillon	1 tablespoon chopped parsley
(if stock not used)	

1. Slice the carrots, potato, and onion. Put them into the soup pot, add the water, bouillon, tomato paste, butter, and sugar. Stir well and cook slowly, covered, over low heat for about 1 hour.
2. When the soup is done, pour it through a strainer, gently rubbing the vegetables through it (or blend in a blender).
3. Reheat the soup. Add salt, pepper, and heavy cream. Stir thoroughly. Serve the soup immediately, garnishing the top with parsley.

In France, the carrots grown in the vicinity of Crécy have the reputation as the best and the tastiest in the whole country – hence the name given to the soup. From France, the soup crossed the Channel into England, where it has become part of the national folklore. According to an old tradition dating back to the 14th century, loyal Britons should eat carrot soup or "potage de Crécy" on the anniversary (August 26, 1346) of the battle of Crécy, a legendary victory of the English over the French in the Hundred Years' War.

Cold Courgette Soup

6 medium-sized courgettes   ½ cup (2 oz, 50g) pesto
1 leek   1 8 oz, (225g) container plain yogurt
1 teaspoon salt   fresh basil leaves and extra yogurt as garnish
2 pts, (1.2 l) water   3 tablespoons lemon juice

1. Slice the courgettes thinly and the leek julienne style. Place them in a soup pot, add the salt and water, and bring them to boil.
2. Boil the vegetables for about 10 minutes and simmer them for another minute. Allow the soup to cool, then add the lemon juice, pesto, and yogurt.
3. Blend the soup in the blender. Refrigerate until the time of serving. Serve soup chilled, with 1 teaspoon of yogurt at the centre, surrounded by leaves of fresh basil as garnish.

I have served this soup many times as an appetizer during midsummer when the first tender courgettes begin to arrive in the garden, and when there seems to be an abundance of basil, of the several varieties our garden produces unfailingly. The soup always receives glowing approvals. For this particular recipe, I like to use the lemony kind of basil, which enhances the, flavour of the soup.

Spicy Carrot and Orange Soup

Ingredients   *6 serving*

6 tablespoons olive oil
2 leeks (white part only), finely chopped
12 carrots, peeled and chopped
1½ cups orange juice
2.5 pts, (1.4 l) vegetable
  or chicken stock
½ teaspoon nutmeg

½ teaspoon paprika
pinch each cayenne and ginger
1¾ oz, (45g) fresh corriander,
  finely chopped
rind of 1 orange
salt and pepper to taste
6 thin orange slices as garnish

1. Pour the oil into a good-sized soup pot and gently sauté the leeks for about 2 minutes with the pot covered. Add the chopped carrots, stir well, cover the pot, and continue cooking for about 4 to 5 minutes over low heat.

2. Uncover the pot, stir once more, and add the stock, nutmeg, paprika, cayenne, ginger, corriander orange rind, orange juice, salt, and pepper to taste. Bring the soup to boil. Cover the pot and let the soup simmer for 30 to 40 minutes.

3. Allow the soup to cook and then pass it through a sieve or blend in a blender or food processor. This soup can be refrigerated for a few hours and served cold, or if you decide to serve it hot reheat it just before serving and let the soup stand for 3 minutes. Garnish the soup with the orange slices at the centre of each serving.

124

Wild Rice Soup

1 pt 14 fl oz, (960ml) vegetable
  or chicken broth
8.5 fl oz, (240ml) dry sherry
1¾ oz, (45g) chopped chervil
  or parsley
2 oz, (50g) mushrooms, sliced
8 oz, (225g) wild rice

salt and white pepper to tast
4 fl oz, (120ml) single cream
4 fl oz, (120ml) water
3 shallots, finely chopped
2 teaspoons freshly chopped thyme
pinch of dry mustard

1. In a soup pot, pour the broth, sherry, and water and bring to a light boil.
    Add the shallots, mushrooms, wild rice, salt, and white pepper. Reduce the heat to
    medium. Cover the pot and cook slowly for 35 to 40 minutes.
2. Check to see that the rice is well cooked; if not, cook for another 5 minutes or so.
    Check the seasonings also. Add more broth if necessary.
3. Add the cream, chervil, thyme, and pinch of dry mustard. Stir the soup thoroughly.
    Cover the pot and simmer the soup for another 10 minutes. Serve immediately,
    or refrigerate it for 2 hours and serve cold.

"The making of a good soup is quite an art, and many otherwise clever cooks do not possess the tour de main necessary to its successful preparation. Either they over-complicate the composition of the dish, or they attach only minor importance to it, reserving their talents for the meal itself, and so it frequently happens that the soup does not correspond to the quality of the rest of the dishes; nevertheless, the quality of the soup should foretell that of the entire meal."

– Mme. Seignobos, *How to Train a Cook*

126

September

"There is no need to bewail the declining year.
Autumn is a glorious season in its own right,
and as pleasant as summer to spend in the garden.
The weather has to remain kind for this to come true,
but the same can be said of any month or season . . .
A gale in September may leave sad,
tattered remnants in its wake,
but if the weather mends, the garden still retains
enough resilience itself to mend."

– Christopher Lloyd

Cream of Celery Soup

Ingredients   *4 servings*

1 garlic clove
6 celery stalks from the heart
2 leeks or onions
2 potatoes

3 pts, (1.7 l) water
8.5 fl oz, (240ml) white sauce
salt and pepper to taste
chopped dill as garnish

1. Wash, peel, and trim the vegetables. Slice them into thin pieces. Pour the water into a large pot, add the vegetables, and cook slowly, covered, over medium heat for 45 to 60 minutes. Add more water if necessary.

2. In a medium-sized pot, prepare 1 cup (8.5 fl oz, 240ml) of white sauce (see recipe p.194).

3. After the vegetables are cooked, blend the soup in a blender and pour it back into the pot. Add the white sauce and seasonings according to taste. Stir well. Serve hot. Use dill or celery, leave chopped finely as garnish. If served cold, refrigerate the soup for a few hours before serving.

This cream of celery soup is easy to prepare and can be served hot or chilled according to the season of the year. The fresh dill garnish adds flavour and distinction to the soup.

Monastery Quick Vichyssoise

4 tablespoons butter, margarine,
  or oil of choice
4 leeks, finely sliced
4 potatoes, diced
1 bouquet garni (1 bay leaf, 1 sprig
  of thyme and parsley tied together and
  removed before serving the soup)
3 bouillon cubes (if stock not used)

1 pt 5 fl oz, (720ml) water
  (or vegetable stock)
17 fl oz, (480ml) milk
salt and fresh pepper to taste
8.5 fl oz, (240ml) double cream (or
  half cream and milk for a lighter option)
fresh parsley or mint leaves for
  garnish (optional)

1. Melt the butter in a large soup pot. Add the sliced leeks and cook them over low heat for about 5 to 6 minutes or until they are tender. Add the potatoes, bouillon, bouquet garni, milk, salt, pepper, and water or stock (you can add more water if necessary).

2. Raise the heat to medium and allow the soup to cook slowly, covered, for 25 to 30 minutes, then simmer for 10 more minutes. Remove the bouquet garni and blend the soup in a blender until thick and creamy. Chill the soup for a couple of hours in the refrigerator. Just before serving, pour the heavy cream into it and stir thoroughly. Serve the soup cold and garnish each plate with finely chopped parsley or mint leaves.

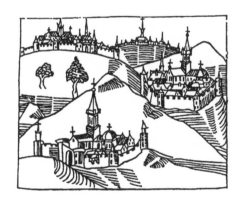

Potage du Jardin
(Garden Vegetable Soup)

Ingredients

3 pts 8 fl oz, (2 l) water
  (or vegetable stock)
2 bouillon cubes (if stock not used)
1 onion
1 courgette
1 carrot

1 celery stalk
3 Swiss chard or cabbage leaves
2 oz, (50g) pastina
salt and pepper to taste
6 tablespoons grated Gruyère cheese

1. Cut the vegetables into small slices julienne style.
2. Place the water in a soup pot. Add the bouillon cubes and vegetables and cook over medium heat for 40 minutes.
3. Add the pastina, salt, and pepper and continue cooking for another 10 minutes.
4. Serve soup hot, and sprinkle grated cheese on top of each serving.

"Gourmet cooking means food that truly satisfies the server: food in which the balance of texture and flavour is exactly right, food that looks and tastes delicious. And contrary to what many people believe, such foods do not have to be elaborate."

– Rose Elliot, *The Festive Vegetarian*

Russian Cream of String Bean Soup

Ingredients   *6 servings*

8 oz, (225g) string beans,
  fresh or frozen
2 leeks, sliced
4 potatoes, peeled and sliced
3 tablespoons butter or margarine

17 fl oz, (480ml) milk
salt and pepper to taste
string beans cut and cooked separately as garnish
finely cut or chopped chives (optional)
2.5 pts, (1.4 l) water

1. Wash and clean the string beans, removing the ends and strings. (Use frozen beans if
    you don't have fresh ones.) Prepare the leeks and potatoes.
2. In a large pot, melt the butter and sauté the vegetables for 1 minute. Stir often.
    Add the water and bring to boil. Lower the heat to low-medium, cover the pot,
    and cook the soup slowly for about 40 minutes.
3. When the vegetables are cooked and tender, pass the soup through a sieve or blend it in
    a blender. Return the soup to the pot and add the milk and seasonings. Stir the soup
    well and bring it again to a light boil. Turn off the heat and let the soup stand for 10
    minutes. Serve the soup hot, and garnish it with small cut string beans that have been
    cooked separately. Some finely chopped or cut chives may be sprinkled on the soup.

Tomato Bouillon

Ingredients   *4 servings*

6 tablespoons oil of choice   2 tablespoons butter
6 tomatoes, peeled   2 tablespoons flour
1 minced onion   3 pts 8 fl oz, (2 l) water
1 bay leaf   salt and pepper to taste
2 peppercorns   double cream (optional)
1 celery stalk, thinly sliced

1. Pour the oil into a soup pot. Add the peeled tomatoes, onion, bay leaf, peppercorns, and celery. Cook slowly (about 15–20 minutes) over low heat until vegetables are cooked. Remove the bay leaf and put the vegetables through a sieve or blend in a blender.
2. Melt the butter in the soup pot, add the flour, and mix well. Add the vegetable mixture, water, salt, and pepper. Heat to boiling point while stirring from time to time, then simmer for 10 minutes. Serve the bouillon hot, adding, if you wish, 1 teaspoon heavy cream to each serving.

"To make a bouillon, one needs time, because quick boiling will not extract the juices and flavours of meats and vegetables: cooking must proceed slowly and be attended to with care."

– F. L. Flagg, *A Paris Cook Book*

Cream of Corn Soup

Ingredients   *4 servings*

1 pt 5 fl oz, (720ml) milk
7 oz, (200g) cooked
  whole-kernel corn
1 large onion, chopped
10 oz, (300g) cooked potatoes
1 teaspoon lemon juice

1/8 teaspoon Tabasco sauce (more or
  less according to taste)
8.5 fl oz, (240ml) single cream
1/4 teaspoon marjoram
salt and white pepper to taste

1. Pour the milk into a blender. Add the corn, onion, potatoes, lemon juice, and Tabasco sauce. Mix in a blender at high speed for a few seconds.
2. Pour the contents of the blender into a soup pot and bring to boil while stirring continually. Add the cream and seasonings. Stir well and simmer for a few minutes before serving.

"Never blow your soup if it is too hot,
but wait until it cools.
Never raise your plate to your lips,
but eat it with your spoon."
– C. B. Hartley, *The Gentleman's Book of Etiquette*

Tomato Soup Florentine Style

Ingredients   *4 serving*

4 fl oz, (120ml) olive oil
1 large onion, finely sliced
7 medium-sized tomatoes, peeled
  and chopped
2 garlic cloves, minced
1 celery stalk, thinly sliced
2 carrots, thinly sliced
2 tablespoons fresh basil, chopped

1 bay leaf
1 teaspoon dried thyme (or fresh)
2 bouillon cubes
2.5 pts, (1.4 l) water (or chicken stock)
1 bunch fresh spinach, chopped (or 1 package
  frozen spinach)
salt and pepper to taste
Parmesan or Romano cheese, grated

1. Heat the oil and add the onions and tomatoes. Sauté the vegetables slightly for 3 to 4 minute. Add the garlic cloves, celery, carrots, basil, bay leaf, and thyme. Stir well and continue sautéing for another 2 minutes.
2. Add the bouillon cubes and water or the stock and bring the soup to boil.
    Cover the pot and simmer the soup for 50 to 60 minutes. Remove the bay leaf.
3. Add the spinach, salt, and pepper and continue cooking for another 10 minutes.
    Stir well. Turn off the heat, and let the soup stand, covered, for 5 minutes.
    Serve hot and sprinkle some grated cheese on top.

Fennel, Courgette and Tomato Soup

Ingredients   *6 servings*

1 large onion, chopped
3 fl oz, (80ml) olive oil
4 garlic cloves, minced
2 fennel bulbs, thinly sliced
2 medium-sized courgettes, diced
6 tomatoes, peeled, seeded,
   and chopped

8 fresh basil leaves, finely chopped
2.5 pts, (1.4 l) chicken or vegetable
   stock (or water)
8.5 fl oz, (240ml) white wine
salt and pepper to taste
fresh basil chopped as garnish

1. Sauté the onion in olive oil until it becomes soft. Add the garlic and continue sautéing
    for another minute over medium heat.
2. Add the fennel, courgettes, tomatoes, and fresh basil. Stir well, reduce the heat to
    low-medium, and continue to sauté for 2 or 3 minutes, watching that it does not stick to
    the bottom of the pot.
3. Pour the stock or water into the vegetable mixture. Add the wine and bring the soup to
    boil. Stir well. Cover the pot and cook slowly for 30 minutes. Add the salt and
    pepper, stir again, and simmer the soup for 10 minutes more. Serve the soup hot.
    Garnish the top of each serving with fresh basil, finely chopped.

*This recipe is quintessentially Italian, inspired as it is by the cuisine of
Northern Italy, where fennel, courgettes, and basil are basic everyday
ingredients in cooking. The soup has a light, subtle liquorice flavour given by
the fennel, and for those who love fennel, it is absolutely delicious. It can be
prepared all year round, but it should be made particularly during the
summer and harvest months when the ingredients can be picked fresh from
the garden.*

Provençal Rainbow Soup

1 onion

2 cloves garlic

1 red pepper

2 small courgettes

20 green beans

1 4 oz, (100g) can pitted
black olives

2 anchovy fillets

8 leaves fresh mint

4 teaspoons olive oil

4 oz, (112g) bacon, cut in small pieces

6 tomatoes, peeled and seeded

1 pt 14 fl oz, (1 l) chicken stock

1 pt 14 fl oz, (1 l) water

salt and pepper to taste

1. Peel the onion and garlic and slice them finely. Cut the red pepper and the courgettes in small cubes. Cut the green beans into three or four parts. Slice the black olives. Put the anchovy fillets and the mint leaves through a food processor or blend in a blender.

2. Pour the olive oil into a large soup pot. Add the bacon, onion, and garlic and cook for 3 minutes over medium heat. Add the other vegetables, olives, and anchovy-mint mixture. Reduce the heat to low and continue cooking for 8–10 minutes, stirring from time to time.

3. Add the sliced tomatoes, chicken stock, water, salt, and pepper. Cover the pot, raise the heat to medium, and let the soup come to boil. Cook for 20 minutes. Turn heat down and let the soup simmer for another 10 minutes. Serve hot.

This potage has all the charm and wonderful aroma that one associates with the native dishes of the rich land of Provence. The variety of colours in the vegetables, which include black olives, is the origin of the soup's charming name. This variety adds not only colour, but also taste and

Gumbo Potage à la Creole

Ingredients

3 fl oz, (90ml) olive oil
2 onions, chopped
2 garlic cloves, chopped
2.5 pts, (1.4 l) chicken or fish stock
17 fl oz, (480ml) dry white wine
1 6oz, (175g) can tomato paste

30 green string beans, cut small
8 okra, sliced
1 carrot, thinly sliced
2 tablespoons brown sugar
1¾ oz, (45g) fresh parsley, chopped
salt and pepper to taste

1. Pour the oil into a large soup pot. Add the onion and garlic. Sauté them over low heat for 2 minutes, stirring often – be sure the garlic does not brown.
2. Add the stock, wine, and tomato paste. Stir well, raise the heat to medium, and bring the soup to a boil.
3. Add the green beans, okra, carrot, sugar, parsley, salt, and pepper. Stir and cover the pot. Cook for 30 minutes over medium heat, then lower heat and simmer for 10 minutes more. Serve hot.

This soup comes from old Louisiana, via France, where it was transported by some local early settlers when they returned to France. The recipe henceforth has received some modifications. For instance, okra, which is not cultivated in France, was omitted altogether. In this recipe, we have reintroduced the use of okra, as well as fish stock as an alternative to chicken stock. A dash of cayenne pepper will also make the soup a bit spicier. The use of wine in the soup is a French improvement.

Curried Soybean Soup

Ingredients

4 tablespoons olive oil	½ teaspoon coriander powder
1 onion, chopped	10 oz, (300g) soybeans
2 carrots, peeled and cubed	3 pts 16 fl oz, (2.2 l) vegetable or meat stock
2 garlic cloves, minced	salt and pepper to taste
2 teaspoons curry powder	chopped corriander as garnish

1. Pour the oil into a soup pot, add the onion and carrots, and sauté them lightly for 2 or 3 minutes. Add the garlic, curry, and coriander and stir thoroughly.
2. Add the soybeans and stock and bring the soup to boil. Reduce the heat, cover the pot, and simmer the soup for 60 minutes or until the beans are cooked and tender (they should remain solid).
3. Remove 1 cup of the beans from the soup and blend it in a blender or food processor, then return it to the soup. Add salt and pepper and stir the soup thoroughly. Serve hot, with chopped corriander on top as garnish.

Minestra Toscana

(Tuscan-Style Minestrone)

4 fl oz, (120ml) olive oil
1 large yellow onion, chopped
2.5 pts, (1.4 l) vegetable
  or chicken broth
17 fl oz, (480ml) white wine
1 bouquet garni (sprigs of thyme,
  oregano, and bay leaf, tied together)
salt and pepper to taste

2 carrots, sliced julienne style
1 red pepper, sliced julienne style
1 courgette, diced
16 spinach leaves, finely chopped
2 oz, (50g) olives (black or green, pitted)
4 oz, (112g) Italian rice or equivalent
grated Parmesan cheese

1. Pour the olive oil into a large soup pot and sauté the onion slightly for about 2 minutes over medium heat.
2. Add the broth, wine, bouquet garni, salt, and pepper and bring the soup to boil. Reduce the heat to low-medium.
3. Add the carrots, pepper, courgette, spinach, and olives. Cover the pot and cook slowly for 1 hour. Add the rice and more broth or water if necessary, and simmer the soup for 15 to 20 minutes more. Remove the bouquet garni. Serve hot and garnish each bowl with grated cheese.

For centuries, the green virgin olive oils of Tuscany have been regarded as the best – "smooth, light, and pleasant on the tongue" said a famous chef. It is precisely these native olive oils that are the base for almost every Tuscan soup. In this soup, the olive fruit is used as well, giving a distinctive flavour, and also enhancing the blend of colours and textures. To achieve this, I recommend the use of black olives, pitted, of course, and sliced in half.

Escarole Soup

Ingredients   *6 servings*

8 tablespoons olive oil
5 garlic cloves, minced
1 onion, finely chopped
1 16 oz, (650g) escarole,
  coarsely chopped
3 pt 8 fl oz, (2 l) water

2 bouillon cubes
4 oz, (112g) vermicelli noodles (or other
  small pasta)
salt and pepper to taste
grated Parmesan cheese as garnish (optional)

1. Pour the oil into a good-sized soup pot, add the garlic and onion, and sauté over
    medium heat for about 3 to 4 minutes, stirring from time to time. Add the escarole and
    continue to stir for another 2 minutes.
2. Add the water and bouillon and cook the soup, covered, over medium heat for 25
    minutes. Add the vermicelli noodles, salt, and pepper and continue cooking for another
    10 minutes, stirring occasionally.
3. Turn off the heat and allow the soup to sit, covered, for 10 minutes before serving.
    You may sprinkle some grated cheese on top of each soup bowl.

140

Red Bean and Rice Soup

Ingredients

3 onions, chopped
3 medium-sized carrots
2 celery stalks
4 tablespoons olive oil
3 pt 8 fl oz, (2 l) water

1 16 oz, (450g) can kidney beans
8 oz, (225g) rice
1 bay leaf
salt and pepper to taste

1. Slice and chop the onions, carrots, and celery. Place them in the soup pot and add the olive oil. Sauté them for 1 or 2 minutes, stirring constantly.
2. Add the water, beans, rice, bay leaf, and seasonings. Cook over medium heat, covered, until the vegetables and rice are tender. Then simmer for 15 minutes more. Remove the bay leaf.
3. Just before serving, bring the soup to the boil again, stir, taste the seasonings, and serve hot.

The purpose of simmering is to cook the ingredients for a long period in order to extract the good flavour, without allowing them to break into particles that would cloud a clear soup to the point that it could not be clarified afterwards because the fat and other particles had been emulsified into the broth.

October

"Suns and skies and clouds of June,
and flowers of June together,
You cannot rival for one hour
October's bright blue weather."

– Helen Hunt Jackson

Brodo alla Romana

(Broth Roman Style)

Ingredients   *4 servings*

3 pts 8 fl oz, (2 l) water
  (add more if necessary)
17 fl oz, (480ml) white wine
2 bouillon cubes
2 large onions, chopped

2 carrots, thinly sliced
3 celery stalks, finely chopped
3 tomatoes, peeled and cubed
salt and pepper to taste

1. Pour the water and wine into a soup pot. Add all the ingredients and let it boil over low-medium heat for 30 minutes.
2. Cover the pot and let the soup simmer for at least 1 hour and 15 minutes. Strain the vegetables and serve the broth hot.

This is a Roman version of the French bouillon, and in typical Italian fashion, it adds tomatoes to the French recipe. The brodo can be thickened and made more substantial by adding either pasta or rice. Garnish it with a bit of extra olive oil and some freshly chopped herbs such as basil, parsley, or thyme.

144

Spinach Soup

Ingredients   *4 servings*

3 pts, (1.7 l) water
1 bunch fresh spinach
6 oz, (180g) sliced mushroom
1 onion, thinly sliced
1 bouillon cube
2 tablespoons flour

8.5 fl oz, (240ml) milk
2 tablespoons oil of choice
  (or butter or margarine)
1 hard-boiled egg, chopped
salt and pepper to taste

1. Bring the water to boil and add the spinach, mushrooms, and onion. Add the bouillon cube. Cook over medium heat for 30 minutes.
2. Stir the flour into the milk, mixing thoroughly. Add this mixture to the soup. Add the oil or butter, the chopped hard-boiled egg, salt, and pepper. Cook for another 10 minutes. Turn off heat and let soup stand, covered, for 5 minutes before serving.

"Rough and repetitious as some soups may be, they are nonetheless delicious if executed by a loving hand and with fresh materials."

— F. L. Stagg, *A Paris Cook Book*

145

Pasta and Lentil Soup

Ingredients 6–8 *servings*

4 fl oz, (120ml) olive oil
1 large yellow onion, chopped
3oz, (75g) chopped mushrooms
4 garlic cloves, minced
3 pts 8 fl oz, (2 l) water
16 oz, (450g) dried lentils
2 8 oz, (225g) cans tomato sauce

1 bay leaf
¼ teaspoon ground ginger
salt and pepper to taste
5 oz, (150g) small pasta shells (or pastina)
grated Parmesan or Romano cheese as
  garnish (optional)

1. Pour the olive oil into a large soup pot. Add and sauté the onions, mushrooms, and garlic over low-medium heat for about 2 or 3 minutes. Stir continually.
2. Add the water, lentils, and tomato paste. Stir well and bring the water to a boil over high heat. Then reduce heat to medium. Add the bay leaf, ginger, salt, and pepper. Stir, cover the pot, and cook the soup for 40 minutes. Remove the bay leaf.
3. Add the pasta, cover the pot, and simmer slowly for 15 minutes or until pasta is cooked. Stir again and serve immediately. Some grated Parmesan cheese may be sprinkled on top of each serving.

"To be a maker of good soups one must not only have skill and patience, but must also use good materials . . . Soup should be palatable and nutritious. If these qualities be lacking, there will be no excuse for serving it. Knowledge and care must be applied in combining the various ingredients in order to secure results at once pleasing and healthful."

– Maria Parloa, *Miss Parloa's Kitchen Companion*

Traditional Austrian Cheese Soup

Ingredients

4 tablespoons oil
2 finely sliced, celery stalks
2 leeks, sliced
2 large potatoes cut into cubes

8 oz, (225g) cream cheese cut into cubes
8 oz, (225g) plain yogurt
salt and pepper to taste
2.5 pt, (1.4 l) water

1. Pour the oil into a soup pot, add the celery, leeks, and potatoes, stirring constantly, for about 2 minutes. Add the water and bring to boil. Lower the heat to medium, cover the pot, and cook the soup slowly for 35 to 40 minutes.

2. When the soup is done, reduce the heat and simmer for 10 minutes, stirring from time to time. Add the cream cheese, yogurt, salt, and pepper. Stir continuously until these latter ingredients melt and blend thoroughly with the rest of the soup. Serve hot.

"Eat soup first and eat it last, and live till a hundred years be past."
– French Proverb

Saint Seraphim Soup

Ingredients   *4 servings*

4 tablespoons butter or margarine   1 onion, sliced
  (or oil of choice)   1 green pepper, cut into small pieces
8 oz, (225g) rice   2 tablespoons chopped parsley
3 pts, (1.7 l) boiling water   salt and pepper to taste
1 large carrot, grated   sprinkle of saffron

1. Melt 4 tablespoons butter in a large soup pot and add the cup of rice to it, stirring continuously for 1 or 2 minutes.
2. Immediately add the boiling water, carrot, onion, green pepper, and parsley.
3. Cook the soup over low heat, covered, for about 30 to 40 minutes, until the rice is tender. Add salt and pepper and a sprinkle of saffron for a bit of extra aroma and taste. Let the soup stand, covered, for 10 minutes and serve.

Saint Seraphim (1759–1833), a Russian monk, lived much of his monastic life as a hermit, studying Scripture and the writings of the monastic Fathers and devoting himself to continual prayer. He cultivated a garden, cooked vegetables and bread, and cared for wild animals. His life was similar to that of the Desert Fathers of 4th-century Egypt. In the last years of his life, he left the forest and dedicated himself to spiritual direction after a vision of the Virgin Mary persuaded him to do so. Numerous visitors and a community of nuns found him an insightful and compassionate spiritual father.

Soupe Savoyarde

(Savoyard Cream of Potato Soup)

Ingredients   *4 servings*

2 pts, (1.2 l) chicken stock
4 large potatoes, peeled and sliced
1 pt, (560ml) milk
4 tablespoons butter

2 oz, (50g) grated Gruyère cheese
  (or Parmesan)
salt and pepper to taste
4 slices bread, toasted

1. Pour chicken stock into a soup pot and bring it to boil. Add the potatoes and cook them, covered, over low-medium heat for 30 minutes.
2. Blend the soup in a blender and then pour it back into the soup pot. Add the milk, butter, cheese, salt, and pepper to taste. Mix well and continue cooking until all the cheese is melted.
3. Place a slice of toast at the centre of each soup plate. Pour the hot soup on top of the toast and serve immediately.

This soup, which is easy to prepare, is particularly liked by children. The normal preparation time is about 15 minutes, with another 35 minutes of cooking time. On cold days, this soup is especially welcome at the table.

Ossobuco Soup

Ingredients   *6-8 servings*

4 fl oz, (120ml) olive oil
2 onions, chopped
2 carrots, peeled and cubed
1 heart of celery, thinly sliced
1 pt 5 fl oz, (720ml)
  dry white wine
1 lemon rind, grated
3 teaspoons dry sage or 3 fresh leaves
2 teaspoons rosemary leaves

2 teaspoons thyme
3 garlic cloves
10 pitted green olives
3 pt 8 fl oz, (2 l) stock (vegetable or fish)
18 oz, (225g) Italian rice (or brown rice)
6 teaspoons capers
salt and pepper to taste
fresh Italian parsley, chopped, as garnish

1. Heat the olive oil in a good-sized soup pot, and gently sauté the onions, carrots, and celery for 3 minutes, stirring frequently. Add the wine, cover the pot, and continue cooking for about 10 minutes.
2. Put the lemon rind, sage, rosemary, thyme, garlic, and olives through a food processor. Add this mixture to the soup pot. Blend and stir thoroughly.
3. Add the stock, rice, capers, salt, and pepper as necessary. Stir and cover the pot. Cook the soup over low-medium heat for about 45 minutes. Turn off the heat and let the soup rest, always covered, for 10 minutes. Sprinkle fresh chopped parsley on top of each serving as garnish. Serve hot and pass around a bowl of grated Parmesan cheese for those who wish it.

Southern-Style Vegetable Soup

Ingredients   *4–6 servings*

4 tablespoons butter or margarine
1 onion, sliced
3 pts 8 fl oz, (2 l) water
2 carrots, diced
1¾ oz, (45g) cabbage, thinly sliced
1 celery stalk, sliced
12 string beans, sliced

¾ oz, (45g) peas
2 large potatoes, diced
2 tomatoes, peeled and sliced
salt and pepper to taste
chopped parsley
1 teaspoon sugar

1. Melt the butter in a soup pot. Add the onion and sauté for 2 minutes. Add the water and all the vegetables except potatoes and tomatoes. Cook over medium heat, covered, for 30 minutes.

2. Add the potatoes, tomatoes, and seasonings and continue cooking for 10 minutes more. Simmer for 15 minutes, or until all vegetables are tender. Before serving, add the chopped parsley and mix well. Serve hot.

"Soup is delicious.
Soup is nutritious.
Soup can light the inner fire.
Soup can be hot or cold,
thick or thin.
Soup is healthy,
light and stimulating –
agreeing with almost everyone."

– Bernard Clayton, Jr., *The Complete Book of Soups and Stews*

Beet Soup

6–8 *servings*

4 beets, peeled and diced
2 onions, finely sliced
3 celery stalks, finely sliced
3 pt 8 fl oz, (2 l) water
1 bouillon cube

6 teaspoons olive oil
2 teaspoons sugar
salt and pepper to taste
mixed herbs (dill and scallion tops)
croutons (optional; see recipe p.195)

1. Pour the water into a soup pot and add the sliced vegetables, bouillon cube, oil, and sugar. Begin to cook slowly.
2. After 30 minutes, add salt and pepper and continue cooking slowly for another 10 minutes. Let the soup stand for 15 minutes. Blend the soup in a blender and return it to the pot. Reheat for five minutes.
3. Just before serving, add the mixed herbs and ladle the soup into individual dishes. Garnish the soup with a few croutons in the centre of each serving.

Beets are not an easy vegetable to deal with. Though many people like them, there are just as many, if not more, who dislike thm. Often, this has a little to do with their colour or taste. Beets actually taste quite good, especially when combined with other ingredients like onions.

This soup is quite simple to prepare. It is very important to slice the beets very thin and cut them into small pieces.

Soupe au Pistou

(Provençal Vegetable Soup with Pesto Sauce)

Ingredients   *6–8 servings*

10 oz, (300g) dried white or
  flageolet beans
4 pt 5 fl oz, (2.4 l) water
2 leeks, or onions, chopped
2 carrots, peeled and sliced
3 potatoes, peeled and cubed
2 courgettes, cubed
12 string beans, cut into small pieces
3 tomatoes, peeled and chopped

sprig of parsley, chopped
1 stalk of celery, chopped
salt and pepper to taste

Pistou Sauce:
7 garlic cloves
10 basil leaves
8.5 fl oz, (240ml) olive oil
6 tablespoons grated Parmesan cheese

1. Soak the beans overnight in cold water. Drain them and place them in a large soup pot with at least 10 cups (4 pts 5 fl oz, 2.4 ltr) fresh water. Add all the vegetables and herbs and bring the water to boil. Cover the pot and simmer the soup for about 50 to 60 minutes, or until beans are tender.

2. Add salt and pepper. Stir well and continue simmering for another 10 to 15 minutes. Keep the soup hot and covered until you are ready to serve it.

3. While the soup is simmering, prepare the *pistou* sauce as follows: Mash the garlic cloves in a mortar. Add the basil leaves and continue mashing or pounding with a pestle until they are well mixed. Add the grated cheese and mix well until it turns into a stiff, consistent paste. Place the mixture in a good-sized serving bowl and add the olive oil little by little. Mix well until it reaches an even consistency. (The *pistou* sauce can also be prepared in a blender or food processor.)

4. Serve the soup hot. Pass the *pistou* bowl around, and let each person add the sauce to his or her own plate.

Those who prefer a thicker soup may add half a cup (4 oz, 112g) of vermicelli noodles.

Leek and Potato Soup

Ingredients   *6 servings*

4 tablespoons butter or margarine or
oil of choice
8 leeks, cut into small, round slices
3 pts 8 fl oz, (2 l) water

5 large potatoes, peeled and diced
salt and pepper to taste
chervil or parsley

1. Melt the butter in a large soup pot and add the leeks. Sauté for about 3 minutes, then add the water and diced potatoes. Cook over medium heat, covered, for about 50 to 60 minutes.

2. Add salt and pepper and mash the potatoes in the soup pot. Stir the soup well. As you dish out each serving, sprinkle a bit of minced chervil or parsley on top. Serve the soup hot.

"Well did he love garlic, onions, and eke leeks, and for to drinken strong wine, red as blood."

– Geoffrey Chaucer,
Canterbury Tales

French Cream of Lentil Soup

Ingredients   *4–6 servings*

4 tablespoons olive oil
2 bacon strips, diced
2 leeks, chopped
2 carrots, sliced
7 oz, (200g) lentils
3 pt 8 fl oz, (2 l) water
1 bay leaf
1 sprig thyme

chopped parsley
salt and pepper to taste
1 egg yolk
4 fl oz, (120ml) milk
olive oil
4 garlic cloves, chopped
croutons sautéed in the garlic and oil as garnish

1. Pour the oil into a soup pot, add the diced bacon, and sauté for about 2 minutes until the bacon becomes crisp. Add the leeks and carrots to the bacon mixture. Stir thoroughly and continue the sautéing process for another 2 minutes.
2. Add the lentils, water, bay leaf, thyme, parsley, salt, and pepper. Bring the water to boil, cover the pot, and let the soup simmer over low heat for 1½ hours. In the meantime, place the egg yolk in a deep bowl, add the milk, and blend well with a mixer. Put this mixture to the side.
3. Let the soup cool. Remove the bay leaf and thyme. Then pass the soup through a sieve, or blend in a food processor or a blender. Return the soup to a clean pot and reheat it. When the soup is hot, add the egg mixture. Stir and blend well. Keep the soup covered.
4. In a small frying pan, pour some olive oil and sauté the chopped garlic for a quick minute, stirring continually. Let garlic get golden, but do not let it burn. Add this garlic mixture to the soup. Stir and blend thoroughly. Serve hot, adding some garlicky croutons on top of each serving as garnish.

Corn Soup

Ingredients   *4 servings*

2 onions
2 garlic cloves
4 tablespoons lard or vegetable oil
2 pt, (1.2 l) vegetable
 or chicken broth or water
 and 2 bouillon cubes)

1 red pepper, sliced in small cubes
1 green pepper, sliced in small cubes
3 tablespoons tomato paste
1 8 oz, (225g) package frozen whole kernel corn
salt and pepper to taste

1. Peel, slice, and mince the onion and garlic. Melt the lard in a good-sized pot.
    Sauté briefly the onion and the garlic, until they begin to turn brown.
2. Add immediately the broth (or water and 2 bouillon cubes). Add the red pepper,
    cover the pot, and bring the contents to boil. Lower to medium heat and cook the soup
    for 15 minutes.
3. After 15 minutes of cooking, add the remaining ingredients: green pepper, tomato paste,
    corn, salt, and pepper. Stir the soup several times until all the ingredients are well
    mixed. Cover the pot and continue cooking for another 15 minutes. Serve hot.

November

"Come, ye thankful people, come
Raise the song of harvest-home!
All be safely gathered in,
Ere the winter storms begin;
God, our Maker, doth provide
For our wants to be supplied;
Come to God's own temple come,
Raise the song of harvest-home!"

– Thanksgiving Hymn

157

Okra Soup

1 onion, chopped
6 oz, (180g) okra, sliced
2 celery stalks, chopped
3 pt 8 fl oz, (2 l) water
2 bouillon cubes

2 oz, (50g) rice
3 oz, (75g) corn kernels
4 fl oz, (120ml) tomato juice
salt and pepper to taste
pinch of cayenne

1. Put vegetables into the soup pot and add the water. Bring the water to boil and add the bouillon, rice, corn, tomato juice, and seasonings. Stir well.
2. Cover the pot and cook the soup slowly over low-medium heat for at least 1 hour, stirring from time to time. Then simmer for 15 minutes, check the seasonings, and serve hot.

"To make nutritious, healthful and palatable soup, with flavours properly commingled, is an art which requires study and practice, but it is surprising from what a scant allotment of material a delicate and appetizing dish may be produced."

– *The Buckeye Cookbook*

Potage au Potiron

(Pumpkin Soup)

Ingredients

2.5 pts, (1.4 l) water (more if necessary)
12 oz, (350g) pumpkin, peeled and cubed
2 potatoes, peeled and cubed
2 carrots, large thinly sliced
2 onions, thinly sliced
2 garlic cloves, minced

pinch of tarragon
salt and pepper to taste
1 pt 14 fl oz, (1 l) milk
3 fl oz, (80ml) vegetable oil
1¾ oz, (45g) parsley, finely chopped

1. Pour the 6 cups (2.5 pints, 1.4 litres) of water into a large pot. Add the pumpkin with the potatoes and the carrot and bring to boil. Add the onion, minced garlic, tarragon, salt, and pepper and continue boiling for about 20 minutes. Reduce heat and simmer for another 20 minutes.

2. Blend the soup in a blender and then pour it back into the pot. Add the milk and the oil, stirring well, and over low heat bring the soup to boil again. Simmer for about 10 minutes and serve immediately in well-heated soup bowls, garnishing each with a pinch of parsley.

Portuguese Kale Soup

6 servings

5 oz, (150g) white beans
4 pt 5 fl oz, (2.4 l) water, more if needed
2 large onions, chopped
16 oz, (450g) kale, chopped
2 potatoes, peeled and cubed

1 6oz can tomato paste
1 teaspoon vinegar
4 garlic cloves, minced chorizo chunks
  (optional: for the non-vegetarian)
salt and pepper to taste

1. Soak the beans overnight. Rinse in cold water.
2. Pour the water into a large soup pot and bring it to boil. Add the beans, onions, kale, potatoes, tomato paste, vinegar, chorizo, and garlic. Cook slowly over low-medium heat for 2 hours. Add more water if necessary. Stir from time to time so the soup does not burn on the bottom of the pot.
3. When the soup is done, add the seasonings and stir the soup well. Turn off the heat, cover the soup pot, and let it stand 10 minutes before serving. Serve hot.

To say the least, this is not only a popular soup in Portugal, but also one of the better known Portuguese dishes around the world. I think it is simply marvellous that a rather common and even dull vegetable such as kale is given prominence in this soup. This is a vegetarian version of the original soup, which calls for a spicy sausage, such as chorizo, as a necessary ingredient. In my view, both versions are equally appetizing.

Black Bean Soup

Ingredients

10 oz, (300g) black beans
4 tablespoons butter
1 onion, chopped
2 celery stalks, chopped
3 pt 8 fl oz, (2 l) water

4 oz, (112g) rice
juice of 1 lemon
salt and pepper to taste
2 flour
2 hard-boiled eggs, sliced

1. Soak the black beans overnight. Rinse them in cold water and drain.
2. Place 3 tablespoons butter in the soup pot, add the onion, and sauté for a few minutes. Add the beans, celery, and water. Bring to boil, then reduce heat to low-medium. Cover the pot and cook slowly for 1½ hours. Stir occasionally.
3. When the beans are tender, add the rice, lemon juice, salt, pepper, and more water if necessary. Cover the pot and cook slowly for another half hour.
4. Melt the remaining butter in a separate skillet, add the flour, and mix thoroughly. Add this mixture to the soup and blend well. When serving the soup, garnish the bowls with slices of hard-boiled eggs.

*T*here are many recipes for black bean soup. This is a mild version of it; for the stronger and spicier Mexican–American version, add some chili peppers, garlic, cumin, and corriander. If it is not possible to cook the beans ahead of time, a can of cooked beans may be substituted. The soup may also be garnished with a spoonful of sour cream over each portion instead of the slices of hard–boiled eggs.

Potato and Cheese Soup

Ingredients

4–6 servings

3 tablespoons butter
2 leeks, thinly sliced
4 large potatoes, peeled and diced
2 pt, (1.2 l) water

17 fl oz, (480ml) milk
3.5 oz, (90g) Cheddar cheese, grated
salt and white pepper to taste
paprika

1. Melt the butter in a soup pot. Add the sliced leeks and sauté them for about 2 minutes on low heat. Add the diced potatoes and continue sautéing for another minute while stirring continually.
2. Add the water and cook over moderate heat, covered, for 30 minutes, or until the vegetables are soft.
3. Add the milk, cheese, salt, pepper, and paprika, and bring the soup to boil. Turn off the heat and let the soup, stand, covered, for 10 minutes. Serve hot.

This is an idyllic wintry soup, both light and robust, a happy marriage between the potato and cheese. For a bit of extra strength and flavour, add 1 teaspoon of cognac per serving. Although the soup is particularly appetizing during the winter months, it is also appropriate in early spring and autumn.

White Bean Soup

16 oz, (450g) dry white beans
5 pt, (2.8 l) water
2 onions
2 carrots
2 leeks
1 celery stalk
a few leaves of garden greens
  (spinach, chard, or any other type of green)

4 garlic cloves
6 tablespoons olive oil
2 bouillon cubes
salt and pepper to taste
finely chopped and minced thyme leaves

1. Soak the dry beans in cold water for at least 10 hours. Rinse them well and put them into a large soup pot with water.
2. Cut the onions, carrots, leeks, celery, and garden greens into thin pieces. Mince the garlic well. Add them all to the soup, along with the oil and the bouillon cubes.
3. Cook the soup, covered, over medium heat for about 60 minutes, stirring from time to time. Let the soup sit for about 10 minutes with the lid on.
4. Add salt, pepper, and thyme. Reheat for another 5 minutes and serve hot.

Broccoli Rabe and Bean Soup

Ingredients

4–6 servings

8 tablespoons olive oil

1 large yellow onion, chopped

6 garlic cloves, minced

2 potatoes, peeled and diced

10 oz, (300g) precooked white
beans or 2 cans of the same beans

4 tomatoes, peeled and chopped

3 pt, (1.7 l) water

1 bunch broccoli rabe, finely chopped

salt and pepper to taste

fresh parsley, chopped

grated Parmesan cheese (optional)

1. In a large soup pot, sauté the onion for about a minute or two. Add the garlic and stir continually for 1 minute. Add the potatoes and the tomatoes and cook over low-medium heat for about 5 minutes, stirring often.

2. Add the precooked beans and the water and bring to boil. Add the broccoli rabe and cook the soup, covered, over medium heat for about 30 minutes. Add salt and pepper and simmer the soup for 10 minutes. Ladle the soup into soup bowls, and sprinkle some finely chopped parsley on the top of each. Grated Parmesan cheese may be used as additional garnish.

*B*eans are one of the most important and healthiest staples in our everyday diet and a basic ingredient for many of the world's most delicious soups across all cultures. Beans are also a great source of protein, especially when combined with rice. The one problem faced by bean lovers is gas discomfort. This can be avoided by soaking the beans for several hours and then discarding the water in which they were soaked. Afterward cook the beans in new, clean water. This particular recipe comes from the southern Italian countryside where broccoli rabe is often used in a variety of culinary concoctions. For extra flavour, add a bouillon cube.

Zuppa alla Pavese

(Bread Soup from Pavia)

4 teaspoons butter or margarine
4 slices bread
4 eggs
1 pint 14 fl oz, (960ml) water

2 pt, (1.2 l) meat or stock of choice
  (or 2 pt, (1.2 l) water and 4 bouillon cubes)
black pepper
grated Parmesan cheese

1. Melt the butter in a frying pan and, over a low heat, fry the bread on both sides. Then place one slice in each soup bowl.
2. Bring to boil 4 cups (1 pint 14 fl oz, 960ml) of water in a soup pot, then lower the heat. Break 1 egg at a time and place the entire egg in the boiling water for 3 minutes. With the help of a large slotted spoon, keep the egg whites all around the yolk so that the egg remains firm and whole. Place each egg on top of the bread.
3. Heat the broth (stock) in a soup pot and bring it to boil. Ladle the stock into each bowl, covering well the bread and the egg. Sprinkle some black pepper and grated cheese on top. Serve immediately.

Rice and Ham Soup

Ingredients   *4 servings*

4 slices cooked ham
2 tomatoes, peeled and sliced
1 onion, sliced
4 tablespoons butter or margarine
8 oz, (225g) rice
2.5 pt, (1.4 l) water

1 bouillon cube
sprinkle saffron
salt and pepper to taste
1 teaspoon thyme, preferably fresh (optional)
Romano cheese

1. Cut the ham slices in small pieces. Do the same with the tomato and the onion.
2. Melt the butter in a soup pot. Add the ham, tomato, and onion. Cook over low heat for about 2 minutes maximum. Add the rice and stir well.
3. Add 6 cups (2.5 pints, 1.4 litres) of water and the bouillon cube (or previously prepared bouillon), saffron, salt, pepper, and thyme (optional). Raise the heat to medium and cook slowly for about 30 minutes. Cover the pot and let the soup simmer for a few minutes. Serve hot, sprinkling some cheese on each serving.

Garbure Béarnaise

(Béarn Country Soup)

Ingredients   *4–6 servings*

16 oz, (450g) navy beans
6 pt 15 fl oz, (4.8 l) water
2 leeks, cut julienne style
2 turnips, sliced
1 small carrot, sliced
1 small cabbage, coarsely chopped
20 green beans
6 potatoes, peeled and left whole

bouquet garni (1 bay leaf, 2 sprigs thyme,
    and 4 sprigs parsley, tied together and
    removed before serving)
6 sweet Italian sausages
2 garlic cloves, minced
4 oz, (112g) salt pork (bacon fat)
salt and pepper to taste

1. Soak the navy beans overnight or at least for several hours. Drain and rinse them. Wash and prepare the vegetables. Pour water into a large soup pot and add all the vegetables except the potatoes, bouquet garni (bay leaf, thyme, parsley tied together), and garlic. Cover the pot and cook the soup slowly over low-medium heat for about 1½ hours. Add more water as necessary.

2. Add the whole potatoes, herbs, sausages, garlic and bacon fat and continue cooking slowly for another hour and 15 minutes. At this point, taste the seasonings and add salt and pepper. (It may need very little salt because of the salt pork.) Take out the whole potatoes, sausage, and pork and keep them in a warm place. Simmer the soup for 15 minutes, remove the bouquet garni, and then serve it hot, accompanied by slices of French bread.

3. After the soup, serve the potatoes and the sausages on a separate plate (1 for each person), accompanied by a fresh green salad and more slices of French bread (you may pour some vinaigrette over the potatoes).

Garbure should be served at the table steaming hot, and it should be accompanied by plenty of French bread and red wine.

Swiss Chard and Lentil Soup

4 tablespoons olive oil
3 garlic cloves, minced
1 good-sized onion, thinly sliced
1 large carrot, cubed
5 oz, (150g) lentils
2.5 pt, (1.4 l) water

1 small bunch Swiss chard leaves, finely
 chopped (8 leaves)
2 chicken bouillon cubes (or vegetable)
2 tablespoons balsamic vinegar
salt and pepper to taste

1. Pour the oil into a soup pot and lightly sauté the garlic, onion, and carrot until they become golden.
2. Add the lentils, water, chard, and bouillon cubes. Cover the pot and cook over medium heat for about 30 minutes.
3. Add the vinegar, salt, and pepper. Stir well and simmer the soup for about 10 minutes. Serve hot.

Basic Monastic Garlic Soup

7 tablespoons oil of choice
16 large garlic cloves, minced
2.5 pt, (1.4 l) water or stock
13 fl oz, (360ml) cups white wine
salt to taste

nutmeg to taste
3 egg yolks, beaten
6 slices whole-wheat bread
3 egg whites beaten stiff

1. Pour the oil into a soup pot, add the garlic, and sauté for a few seconds while stirring constantly. Add the water, wine, salt, and nutmeg and bring to boil. Reduce heat to low-medium and continue to cook for 30 minutes. Add the egg yolks, stirring continuously. Simmer for another 15 minutes with the pot covered.
2. When it is time to serve, reheat the soup to boiling. Place 1 slice of bread in each of the six soup bowls. Scatter the stiff egg whites over the bread, then pour 2½ ladles of hot soup on top of each. Serve immediately.

This recipe is a particular version of a soup popular in monasteries and convents of Latin-Mediterranean Europe (Italy, France, Spain, Portugal). Because of its monastic origins, this recipe is rather frugal in character, but it may easily be enriched by using vegetable or chicken stock prepared ahead of time, and also by adding an extra cup of wine.

Potage à l'Oseille

(Cream of Sorrel Soup)

6 tablespoons olive oil
4 leeks (chop only white parts)
1 large onion (well chopped)
2.5 pt, (1.4 l) sorrel,
  coarsely chopped
2.5 pt, (1.4 l) water (more if needed)

2 bouillon cubes
1 bunch parsley, well chopped and minced
salt, pepper, and nutmeg to taste
4 potatoes, peeled and cubed
6 tablespoons double cream

1. In a large stainless-steel pot, lightly sauté the leek and onion in the olive oil. Add the sorrel and the potatoes and stir for a few minutes until the vegetables are well mixed.
2. Add the water; bouillon cubes, parsley, salt, pepper, and nutmeg and boil for about 15 minutes. Simmer the soup in the covered pot for about 20–25 minutes.
3. Blend the soup in a blender and then pour it back into the pan. Add the heavy cream and stir the soup. Reheat and serve hot.

Sorrel plays an important role in French cooking since it has a good delicate flavour and colour. Also, when used correctly, sorrel blends well with other flavours, adding a special richness to many recipes. I am particularly fond of sorrel, not only because of its special taste, but also because of its appealing dark green colour.

December

"Now Christmas is come
Let us beat up the drum,
And call all our neighbours together,
And when they appear,
Let us make them such cheer
As will keep out the wind and the weather."

– Washington Irving

171

Aigo-Boulido
(Herb Bouillon)

Ingredients   *4 servings*

8 tablespoons olive oil
2 leeks, sliced
1 onion, sliced
6 cloves of garlic, minced
2 tomatoes, pureed, seeds discarded
3 pints 8 fl oz, (2 l) water
4 medium potatoes, diced
1 bouquet garni (sprigs of thyme,
  sage, and bay leaf tied together
  and removed before serving)

dash orange peel
pinch saffron (optional)
salt and pepper to taste
4 eggs
4 slices French bread
1 bunch parsley
grated cheese (optional)

1. In a large soup pot, sauté the leek, onion, and garlic in the oil. Add the tomato purée and sauté for another 2 minutes. Add water, potatoes, bouquet garni, orange peel, saffron (optional), salt, and pepper. Cover the pot. Boil for about 25 minutes, and then simmer for another 25 minutes. While the soup is simmering, poach 4 eggs in some of the broth for about 3 minutes. (Strain the soup and discard the vegetables, herbs, etc.)
2. Prepare 4 soup bowls and place a slice of French bread in the centre. Ladle the soup into the bowls and place a poached egg on top of the bread. Sprinkle finely chopped parsley and cheese on top of the soup and serve hot.

"L'aigo-boulido sauvo la vido" ("The boiling water saves life") is an old Provençal saying that refers to one of the great and most popular peasant soups of Provence. Basically, it is a healing and restorative broth of vegetables and herbs. In Provence, it is the most common medicine for colds among both children and grown-ups. It is also often given when one suffers from stomach ailments.

Saint Nicholas Soup

Ingredients

2 oz butter or margarine
2 leeks or onions
4 medium-sized carrots
3 turnips
4 potatoes

half a medium-sized head white cabbage
1 teaspoon salt or more, according to taste
6 pt 15 fl oz, (4 l) water
croutons (see recipe p. 195)
1¼oz, (30g) minced chervil, chopped

1. Wash and peel the vegetables. Slice them into small pieces.
2. Melt the butter in a large soup pot. Add the vegetables and salt and stir a few times. Turn off the heat, cover the pot, and let it rest for about 15 to 20 minutes. Add the water and bring the soup to a boil. Reduce the heat to medium-low, cover the pot, and allow the soup to cook slowly for about 30 to 40 minutes. Stir from time to time.
3. When the soup is done, blend all of it in a blender until it becomes creamy and even. Serve hot, adding some croutons to each bowl and sprinkling some chervil on top.

Zuppa Toscana
(Tuscan Bread and Tomato Soup)

3 fl oz, (90ml) olive oil
1 onion, sliced
4 garlic cloves, minced
1 tablespoon minced fresh rosemary
1 tablespoon minced sage
2 tablespoons thyme

8 tomatoes, peeled (or 2 16 oz, (450g)
  cans of tomatoes)
16 slices stale French or Italian bread
1 pt 14 fl oz, (1 l) vegetable or chicken stock
1 pt 14 fl oz, (1 l) dry white wine
salt and pepper to taste
grated Parmesan cheese

1. Heat olive oil in a large soup pot. Add the onion, garlic and fresh herbs and sauté them for about 1 or 2 minutes. Do not let the onion or garlic turn brown.
2. Add the stale bread slices and continue cooking for a minute or two while stirring all the time. Turn off the heat.
3. In a separate pot, cook the tomatoes for about 4 to 5 minutes. Add the stock and the wine, salt, and pepper and bring to boil. Lower the heat to medium-low. Add the bread mixture and continue cooking for about 12 to 15 minutes. Lower the heat and simmer for another 15 minutes.
4. Serve the soup very hot, sprinkling the grated cheese on top at the last minute.

This delicious peasant soup comes to us from the land of Tuscany. This ancient region of Italy evokes memories of the Renaissance, of art, music, fine wine, and food. This soup is typical of the region, where the abundance of olive oil, wine, and tomatoes, combined with the herbs and country bread, goes to create a most appetizing and flavourful soup. It should be prepared especially during the time of the harvest, when the fresh tomatoes are in abundance. Fresh herbs should be used as much as possible.

Saint Lucy Soup Sicilian Style

6 pt 15 fl oz, (4.l) water
8.5 fl oz, (240ml) olive oil
16 oz, (450g) whole-grain dried wheat
16 oz, (450g) dried chickpeas

8 garlic cloves, minced
2 large onions, sliced
3 bay leaves
salt and pepper to taste

1. Pour the water and oil into a large soup pot. Add the other ingredients and let it boil slowly, covered, for 3 or 4 hours, stirring from time to time.
2. Check the seasonings, remove the bay leaves, and serve the soup hot. Those who wish can sprinkle some Parmesan cheese into their bowls.

This Sicilian soup is named after Saint Lucy (d. 304), one of the patron saints of Sicily. She was born of noble parents near Syracuse, and when she refused to marry a pagan young man, he denounced her as a Christian to the authorities. Sentenced to a brothel, she was made miraculously immobile. Several attempts were made to kill her, including once by fire, but the flames refused to touch her. Finally she was stabbed to death through the throat. Saint Lucy is much loved by the Sicilian people, who often give her name to their baby girls. She is also invoked by people who suffer eye trouble: Legend has it that her own eyes were torn out but miraculously restored.

Yellow Pea Soup

4 tablespoons olive or vegetable oil
2 onions, chopped
1 celery stalk, thinly sliced
1 large carrot, thinly sliced
1 medium-sized turnip, diced
3 pt 8 fl oz, (2 l) water

half a butternut squash,
  peeled and cut into chunks
7 oz, (200g) yellow split peas
1 sprig of thyme
1 bay leaf
fresh parsley, chopped
salt and pepper to taste

1. Pour the oil into a large soup pot. Add the chopped onions and sauté them over moderate heat until the onions turn soft. Add immediately the celery, carrot, and turnip. Stir the vegetables well and continue sautéing for another minute.
2. Add the water, chunks of squash, split peas, thyme, bay leaf, and chopped parsley. Cover the pot and bring the soup to boil.
3. Cook the soup slowly, over medium heat, for 45 to 60 minutes or until the peas are totally dissolved. Add salt and pepper. Stir well and simmer the soup for 10 minutes. Remove the bay leaf and serve hot.

The appeal of this soup lies in its taste, colour, and texture. When the peas are properly cooked and totally dissolved, they turn the soup into a creamy one, yellowish in colour and thick in texture. The morsels from the vegetables also enhance the texture of the soup. This soup can also be put through a food mill or a blender and served as a thick purée. The butternut squash adds a sweet, delicate flavour to the soup and enhances its yellow-orange colour. For a bit of extra taste, add 1 or 2 bouillon cubes. If this soup is prepared for an elegant dinner or for a special occasion, it should be served in the creamy purée form with some fresh minced parsley on top as garnish.

Caldo Gallego

(Galician Chickpea and Sausage Soup)

Ingredients *6 servings*

10 oz, (300g) dried chickpeas or
  2 15 oz, (425g) cans garbanzos
2 large onions, sliced
6 tablespoons olive oil
2 garlic cloves, minced
1 pt 14 fl oz, (1 l) water
12 fresh spinach leaves, chopped
1 bunch fresh parsley, chopped

1 turnip, diced
1 large carrot, diced
2 potatoes, peeled and cut in cubes
1 heart of celery, thinly sliced
8 slices sweet Spanish chorizo, cut in half
4 cups (1 pt 14 fl oz, (1 l) chicken or meat stock
1 bay leaf
salt and pepper to taste

1. Soak the chickpeas overnight and then rinse them and discard the water. If you wish to save time, use the canned chickpeas (garbanzos), which taste the same.
2. In a large soup pot, sauté the onions in the olive oil for 2 or 3 minutes or until they begin to turn soft. Add the garlic and stir well.
3. Add the water and stock. Bring the soup to boil. Add the chickpeas, bay leaf, parsley, turnip, carrot, potatoes, celery, and chorizo. Cook the soup, with the pot covered, for 1 hour and 15 minutes over medium heat or until the chickpeas are tender.
4. Add the chopped spinach, salt, and pepper and simmer the soup gently for 15 to 20 minutes, adding more water if needed. Stir it from time to time. Remove the bay leaf. Turn off the heat and serve the soup hot.

Perhaps Galicia is best known for its ancient town Santiago de Compostela, containing one of the wonders of the world, its famous cathedral, where according to tradition the Apostle James is buried.

A Hermit's Soup

Ingredients   *2 servings*

1 potato
1 turnip
half a small cabbage
2 carrots
1 onion

3 tablespoons oil of choice
3 oz, (75g) rice
3 pt 8 fl oz, (2 l) water
salt and a pinch of thyme to taste

1. Wash and trim the vegetables. Cut and slice all of them into tiny pieces.
2. Pour oil into a soup pot, add the vegetables, and sauté them for a few minutes.
    Add the rice and water. Stir well. Keeping the pot covered, cook over low heat for
    1 hour. Add the salt and thyme just before serving. Stir well and serve hot.

The very nature of this soup is one of great simplicity and frugality, expressing the life of a hermit. This life is one that, in the words of Saint Paul, is "hidden with Christ in God." The hermit monk makes use of basic root vegetables for this soup, such as turnip, carrots, and onions. Added to these are the inexpensive ingredients of cabbage and rice. This soup can be made in sufficient quantities to last for a few days.

Simple Onion Soup

Ingredients   *4–6 servings*

16 oz, (450g) beef bones for stock
5 pt, (2.8 l) water
2 tablespoons flour or cornstarch
4 fl oz, (120ml) milk

6 onions, coarsely sliced
3.5 oz, (90g) grated Gruyère,
   Parmesan, or Romano cheese
salt and pepper to taste

1. Place the bones in a large pot. Add water and bring to a high boil. Lower the heat, cover the pot, and continue boiling for 3 hours. Let the stock cool and remove the bones.
2. Take the fat from the top of the stock and place it in another casserole. Add the flour, milk, and half a cup stock. Dissolve well and cook the mixture for about 2 minutes, stirring continually.
3. Add the mixture to the soup, and also the sliced onions. Stir well and bring the soup to a second boil. Cover the pot and cook for about 30 minutes over low-medium heat. Turn off the heat, add the grated cheese, stir well, cover the pot, and let the soup stand for 5 minutes. Serve hot.

The very essence of this soup consists in its rich, long–laboured, homemade stock. It blends wonderfully with the onions without overpowering the soup with a strong meaty and salty flavour. This soup is particularly welcome on a chilly day. It warms both body and soul.

Zuppa Vesubio

(Vesuvio Vegetable-Cheese Soup)

Ingredients *5–6 servings*

3 pt, (1.7 l) vegetable or meat stock
4 potatoes, peeled and diced
4 carrots, peeled and thinly sliced
3 fl oz, (90ml) olive oil

2 red peppers, diced
salt and pepper to taste
8 oz (225g) Mozzarella cheese,
  as fresh as possible
2 onions

1. Pour the stock into a soup pot and add the potatoes and carrots. Cook until the vegetables are tender. Pass the vegetables through a sieve or blend in a blender.
2. Pour the olive oil into a separate pot and sauté the onions for 3 or 4 minutes. Add the diced peppers and continue sautéing for another minute or two. Add the potato-carrot mixture and salt and pepper and cook, covered, over low-medium heat for about 20 minutes.
3. Cut the Mozzarella cheese in thin slices and add them to the soup. Ladle the soup into six bowls. Place the bowls in a hot oven (350°) until the cheese melts well into the soup. Serve immediately.

Soybean Minestra

6 tablespoons olive oil
4 ripe tomatoes, peeled
4 garlic cloves
4 parsley sprigs
2 leeks, chopped
8 leaves sorrel or spinach
4 pt 5 fl oz, (2.4 l) water

1 carrot, sliced
1 celery stalk, sliced
7 oz, (200g) soybeans
10 string beans, cut small
1 ham bone (optional), or 2 bouillon cubes
salt and pepper to taste
2 potatoes, cubed

1. Pour olive oil into large soup pot. Pass the peeled tomatoes, garlic cloves, and parsley through a small food processor or blend in blender. Put the mixture in the soup pot and cook slowly over medium heat.
2. Add the chopped leeks, sorrel, and 2 cups (17 fl oz, 480ml) water. Bring to boil and cook for about 10 minutes. Add the potatoes cut into cubes, the sliced carrot, celery, soybeans, string beans, ham bone, and 8 cups (3 pints 8 fl oz, 2 litres) of water (more if needed).
3. Cover the pot and cook slowly for 1½ hours over low-medium heat. Turn off the heat and add salt and pepper. Let the soup sit for about 15 minutes. Serve hot.

Soybeans are very nutritious, but they don't seem to have much flavour. However, the blend of soybeans and all the other vegetables in this soup creates a delicious and very distinctive taste, similar to a minestrone. To make a complete meal out of it, add 1 cup (8 oz, 225g) of rice, and for extra zest and taste, add 1 cup (8.5 fl oz, 240ml) dry white wine.

Gloucester English Cheese Soup

4 tablespoons butter or margarine
2 leeks, shredded julienne style
2 celery stalks, sliced julienne style
2 medium-sized carrots, sliced
  julienne style
1 turnip, sliced julienne style
1 potato, diced
1 bouquet garni (parsley, thyme, and
  bay leaf tied together)

3 garlic cloves, minced
2 bouillon cubes
2.5 pt, (1.4 l) water
8.5 fl oz, (240ml) low-fat milk
salt and pepper to taste
7oz, (200g) Gloucester cheese, shredded
chopped parsley as garnish

1. Melt the butter in a large soup pot and gradually add all the vegetables. Stir well, cover the pot, and cook slowly over low heat for about 10 minutes.
2. Add the bouquet garni and the garlic cloves, stir again, and continue cooking for an additional 2 minutes. Add the bouillon cubes, water, milk, salt, and pepper. Stir thoroughly, cover the pot, and cook for 45 minutes over medium heat.
3. Turn off the heat, discard the bouquet garni, and blend the soup in a blender or food processor.
4. Return the soup to the pot. Reheat the soup at low to medium heat and add the shredded cheese. Simmer the soup for 10 minutes and serve it hot. Garnish the soup with finely chopped parsley and some extra shredded cheese.

This very tasty soup originates, as the name proclaims, from Gloucester, England, where the well-renowned Gloucester cattle produce an abundance of milk, some of which in turn is made into the famous Gloucester cheese. If this particular cheese is not available, substitute with another English cheese, preferably of the blue variety.

Beer Soup

Ingredients

5 cans beer of choice
2 tablespoons sugar
4 egg yolks
6 tablespoons crème fraîche (or double cream)

½ teaspoon cinnamon
½ teaspoon salt
black pepper to taste

1. Pour all the beer into a large soup pot. Add the sugar and dissolve it slowly in the beer over low-medium heat. Bring to boil and then remove the soup pot from the heat.
2. Beat the egg yolks in a deep bowl, adding the crème fraîche (or cream), a little bit at a time. Add 4 tablespoons hot beer to the egg mixture and blend well.
3. Pour the egg mixture into the soup pot containing the hot beer. Add cinnamon, salt, and pepper. Reheat the soup over low heat and stir constantly. Allow the soup to cook for a few minutes without bringing it to boil. Serve soup hot.

"Cooking is also of all the arts the one that has done most to advance our civilization, for the needs of the kitchen were what first taught us to use fire, and it is by fire that man has tamed nature itself."
– Anthelme Brillat-Savarin

Acorn Squash Soup

2 large acorn squash	16 fl oz, (480ml) milk
1 large onion, chopped	4 tablespoons vegetable oil
8 oz, (225g) rice	pinch sugar
1 celery stalk, chopped	salt and white pepper to taste
1 pt 14 fl oz, (1 l) water	chopped parsley

1. Peel the squash and cut it into cubes. Place them in a soup pot and add the chopped onion, rice, chopped celery, and water. Cook the soup, covered, over medium heat until vegetables are tender.

2. Strain the soup through a sieve or blend it in a blender. Reheat soup and add the milk, oil, sugar, salt, and pepper. Stir and bring to boil, then simmer for 2 to 3 minutes. Sprinkle with parsley just before serving. Serve hot.

*T*his is a lovely soup for wintertime. Acorn squash keeps well in our cellars during the winter, and it is a joy to make use of them in different ways in the kitchen. The taste and texture of the acorn squash enhances the quality of the soup. If the soup is a bit too thick, add some extra water.

Egg Soup

Ingredients

2 large onions, chopped and minced
6 tablespoons olive oil
2.5 pt, (1.4 l) strong vegetable stock
16 fl oz, (480ml) dry white wine

4-6 well-beaten eggs (1 per person)
salt and pepper to taste
a pinch of cayenne (optional)
1¾ oz, (45g) chopped chervil

1. Pour the oil into a soup pot, add the onions, and cook them slowly for a few minutes. Stir and do not let them get brown.
2. Add the vegetable stock and the wine. Cover the pot and bring to boil, then simmer for 10 to 15 minutes.
3. Beat the eggs and add them to the soup. Add the salt, pepper, and cayenne. Reheat the soup, stir, but do not bring to boil. Serve immediately and sprinkle some chervil on the top of each serving as garnish.

This is a versatile, quick, and easy-to-prepare soup. To me, it is a rather nostalgic soup, for it captures some of the fond memories of early childhood when my parents or grandparents would give us children egg soup when we were sick, so that being properly nourished, we would recover quickly. Because this is such a simple and basic soup, condiments (onions, cayenne pepper, chervil, etc.) are absolutely necessary in order to give flavour to the soup.

Mushroom Soup

6 medium-sized potatoes
20 mushrooms, preferably the dried type
4 fresh parsley sprigs
4 garlic cloves, minced

4 tablespoons butter or margarine
2.5pt, (1.4 l) boiling water
salt and pepper to taste
10 teaspoons crème fraîche

1. Wash and peel the potatoes. Cut them into cubes. Wash and slice the mushrooms thinly and evenly. Peel and mince the garlic and parsley.
2. Melt the butter in a large saucepan. Add the potatoes and mushrooms and cook them over medium heat for about 3 minutes, stirring often. Add the garlic, parsley, salt, and pepper and mix well.
3. Add boiling water and cook the soup for 1 hour. (Add more water if needed.)
4. Just before serving, add the crème fraîche and blend thoroughly. Serve hot.

This is a delicious, easy-to-prepare, and very economical soup. If possible, one should try to use cépes, the dried type of mushrooms that are used in France. If they are not available, ordinary mushrooms will do. The same can be said for crème fraîche – if it is not available locally, you may substitute an equal amount of sour cream.

Potage aux Deux Légumes

(Celery-Carrot Soup)

Ingredients

4 servings

3 carrots
1 heart of celery
2 pt, (1.2 l) chicken stock

salt and pepper to taste
parsley as garnish

1. Wash and slice vegetables thinly.
2. Pour the stock into a soup pot and bring it to boil.
3. Add the sliced vegetables, salt, and pepper, and cook over medium heat for 15 to 20 minutes. Serve hot. Sprinkle some fresh minced parsley over each plate.

This is an easy soup to prepare in an emergency situation, when one has little time to go through a more complicated recipe. It is a particularly good soup for children. I recommend that the carrots and celery be sliced thinly lengthwise, as for french-fried potatoes.

Appendix:
Basic Recipes for Stocks, Sauces and Croutons

Meat Broth

Ingredients

about 10 cups

6 pts 16 fl oz, (4 l) water (more if necessary)
2 pounds (900g) beef bones, shoulder,
  top ribs, etc. (any bones and meat that
  can be spared are good)
2 leeks, sliced
2 onions, sliced
2 carrots, sliced
1 celery stalk, sliced

4 garlic cloves, minced
2 bay leaves
1 sprig of thyme (or 1 teaspoon dried)
4 whole cloves
8 black peppercorns
6 sprigs parsley
salt to taste
2 potatoes, peeled and sliced

1. Pour the water into a large soup pot and add the meat, bones, vegetables, and all the
   spices. Bring it to boil. Reduce the heat and simmer the broth for about 3 to 4 hours,
   stirring it from time to time. Cover the pot.
2. After the long simmering, when the broth is done, remove the bones and meat.
   Pass the broth through a thin strainer, which should collect all the vegetables and spices
   and leave the broth clear.
3. Serve the broth hot as such, or refrigerate and use it later as the base for other soups.
   It can also be put in the freezer to keep it for future use.

Consommé

Ingredients   *4 servings*

2.5 pt, (1.4 l) meat broth
  (see recipe on previous page)
670g minced lean beef
1 carrot, sliced
1 leek, sliced

1 bouquet of celery leaves and
  parsley sprigs well tied
1 egg white, well beaten
salt and pepper to taste

1. Pour the broth into a large soup pot. Add the meat, vegetables, bouquet of celery and parsley, and egg white. Stir well the ingredients in the broth and bring it to boil.
2. Lower the heat to low-medium, stir some more, add salt and pepper, cover the pot, and let the consommé cook slowly for about an hour and a half.
3. Filter the consommé through a very fine strainer or cheesecloth, and then serve it very hot. This consommé can be served as an appetizer to a very fine and elegant dinner.

Vegetable Broth

Ingredients   *about 12 cups (5 pints, 2.8 litres)*

7 pints 13 fl oz, (4.3 l) water
  (add more if necessary)
3 carrots, sliced
2 turnips, sliced and diced
2 courgettes, sliced
2 leeks, sliced
1 onion, coarsely chopped
2 celery stalks, sliced

1 small lettuce, coarsely chopped
  (or a few leaves of cabbage)
4 bay leaves
1 orange peel, minced
a few parsley sprigs, tied together
black peppercorns to taste
salt to taste

1. Pour the water into a large soup pot and add all the ingredients mentioned above.
    Bring the water to boil and keep it boiling for about 30 minutes. Stir from time to time.
2. Reduce the heat to low-medium, stir some more, cover the pot, and let the broth simmer
    for about 2 hours. Filter the broth through a fine sieve, strainer, or cheesecloth.
    Allow it to cool and then store it in the refrigerator or freezer for future use.
    This bouillon is a wonderful remedy in case of colds and stomach troubles.

Chicken Broth

Ingredients   *about 12 cups (5 pints, 2.8 litres)*

7 pt 13 fl oz, (4.3 l) water
2 pounds (900g) chicken pieces
  (or more if available)
2 onions, coarsely chopped
2 leeks, thinly sliced
2 carrots, sliced
1 celery stalk, sliced

5 garlic cloves, minced
1 bay leaf
1 egg white, beaten
a bouquet of thyme and parsley sprigs, tied
black peppercorns to taste
salt to taste

1. Pour the water into a good-sized soup pot and add all the ingredients mentioned above.
    Bring the water to boil, stir thoroughly, and then reduce the heat to low-medium.
    Cook slowly for about 2 hours and add more water if necessary.
2. When the broth is done, turn off the heat and let it rest gently for about 45 minutes.
    Withdraw the chicken and vegetables and then ladle the broth through a very fine
    strainer, or even better, through cheesecloth. When the broth has cooled, place it in
    proper plastic containers and store it in the freezer for future use.

Fish Broth

About 12 cups (5 pints, 2.8 litres)

Follow the recipe for Chicken Broth, but substitute fish bones, tails, etc., for the chicken
pieces and add all the juice of a whole lemon. The best type of fish to use for broth
making are red snapper, cod, haddock, and striped bass. It takes less time to make fish
broth, so 1½ hours of slow cooking is enough for the making of a fine broth or stock.

White Sauce

2 tablespoons cornflour or flour
1½ cups milk
2 tablespoons butter or margarine

salt and black pepper to taste
dash of nutmeg

Dissolve the cornflour into half a cup of milk. Melt the butter in a medium-sized stainless-steel pot over medium heat. When the butter begins foaming, add the milk and cornstarch and stir continuously. Add the rest of the milk, salt, pepper, and nutmeg and continue to stir until the sauce comes to boil. Lower the heat and continue stirring until the sauce thickens. The sauce is ready when it is smooth and thick. The sauce can be used as a base for many other useful variations. It can be used on fish, meats, eggs, vegetables, and soups.

Béchamel Sauce

2 tablespoons butter or margarine
2 tablespoons cornstarch or flour
16 fl oz, (480ml) milk

1 tablespoon dry sherry (optional)
salt and pepper to taste
pinch of nutmeg (optional)

Melt the butter in a good-sized stainless-steel pot over medium-low heat. Add the cornstarch and stir continuously with a whisk. Add the milk little by little while whisking continuously. Add the sherry, salt, pepper, and nutmeg and continue stirring. When it begins to boil, reduce the heat and continue cooking slowly until it thickens. This sauce is excellent with fish and vegetables, and it is a necessary base for soufflés, omelettes, and other egg dishes.

Croutons

6 tablespoons olive oil
6 slices French bread
(or Italian, or any other of
your choice), sliced in cubes

dash each of dried thyme and dried parsley
2 garlic cloves, minced

1. Pour the oil into a pot, add the garlic, bread cubes, and herbs and sauté them over low heat for 3 to 5 minutes. Stir and turn constantly.
2. Remove the croutons and keep them in a lightly warm oven until you are ready to use them. Croutons are especially useful as garnish in thick, creamy soups.

"Soup sought is good,
but given unsought is better."
– Old Proverb

195

Index